ROUTE
AND
BRANCH

North East England

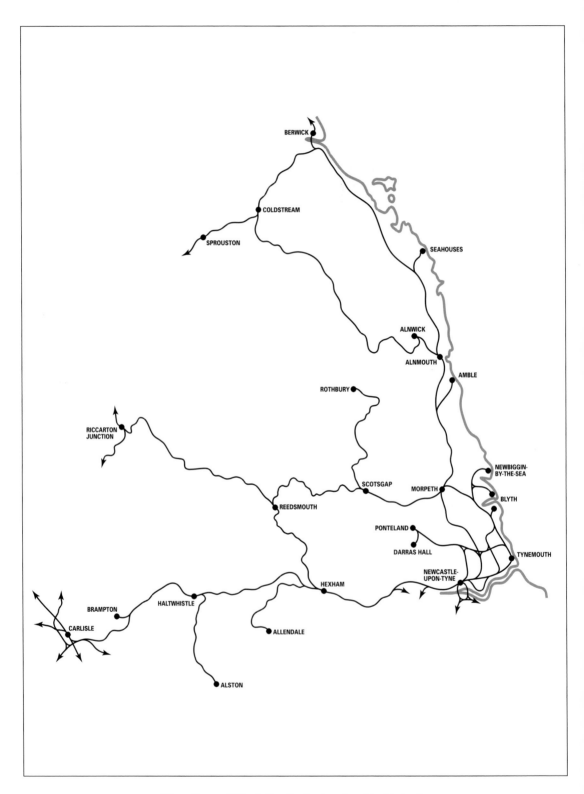

The railways of North East England explored in this book.

ROUTE
AND
BRANCH

A personal exploration of the railway heritage of
North East England

Mike Griggs

· RAILWAY HERITAGE ·

from

The NOSTALGIA Collection

First published in 2006

British Library Cataloguing in Publication Data

A catalogue record for this book is available from the British Library.

ISBN 1 85794 265 5
ISBN 978 85794 265 1

Silver Link Publishing Ltd
The Trundle
Ringstead Road
Great Addington
Kettering
Northants NN14 4BW

Tel/Fax: 01536 330588
email: sales@nostalgiacollection.com
Website: www.nostalgiacollection.com

Printed and bound in Great Britain

All Ordnance Survey maps are Crown copyright, by permission of the Syndics of Cambridge University Library.
All historic photographs are from the Neville Stead collection, with the photographer's name given where appropriate.
All modern-day photographs are by the author.

▼ A crossing-keeper's cottage just north of the former Belford station on the East Coast Main Line

▶ Ewesley station on the Rothbury branch: the platform remains, looking south (see page 32)

CONTENTS

Northumberland contrasts: the East Coast Main Line at the site of Little Mill station north of Alnmouth; a colliery branch north of Ashington; and Twizell station on the Berwick-Coldstream line, with the remains of the platform in the vegetation on the left.

INTRODUCTION

This is not a book solely about railways but a descriptive narrative of five intensive tours made to the Northumberland area almost 10 years ago. It resembles in many ways an extended treasure-hunt as each objective had to be found, assessed and usually photographed in a short space of time. Careful planning beforehand enabled a detailed itinerary to be produced, which included just about every known feature of the old railway system, and although time was of the essence, taking the easy way out was never an option. This volume describes my wanderings and experiences beginning at Carlisle on a sunny June morning in 1996 and ends in May of the following year, on a grey afternoon at Newcastle Central. This, in fact, was only the beginning, as over the next four years virtually all the railways of North East England were explored. The book is essentially a record of what became of the old railway system and includes a selection of older photographs and a number of large-scale maps that highlight some of the more interesting locations.

Years ago it was all so very different as the once grimy, nerve-racking and exhausting pastime of taking engine numbers had taken over my whole life, well before my teenage years. Very soon the hobby became focussed on engine sheds – so great were their

fascination that almost overnight not only had every shed code been memorised, including sub-sheds, but its position determined with the help of the indispensable Shed Directory. Numerous expeditions were undertaken by train and coach but all too soon it was to end as modernisation gathered pace.

By the late 1960s most sensible people had taken up a new hobby, but for some the trips had to continue, only now the sheds were abandoned and decaying. As time passed, a 'let's pretend' scenario developed as enthusiasts continued to pay homage to engine sheds by treading cinder paths to rediscover some shadowy, ruinous building bordering a warren of back streets or perhaps nothing more than a heap of rubble in a verdant wilderness deep in the country. As the years slipped by most of the rustic remains of our railways have disappeared or been adapted for other uses. It was in memory of these wanderings that in 1996 I formulated the possibility of taking to the road to try and visit every place of railway interest in North East England and to record my findings in the form of a book.

More recently the vast array of railway books and other material has made it possible to imagine the railway as it used to be as never before. This book aims to illustrate the initiatives required and difficulties faced when exploring old railways, and is a tribute to all enthusiasts who continue to keep alive our railway heritage and, as much as it is possible, to dream again of the past.

The journey began in Carlisle on a June morning in 1996 and ended within sight of Shaftholme Junction in 2001. Most tours went according to plan, often the scheduled times proving to be almost spot-on: nearly always the whole itinerary was completed. One was always conscious of an unforeseen occurrence such as a car breakdown, accident or minor injury spoiling the continuity of the book. I was lucky as only one tour had to be aborted, due to brake failure not long after leaving home. I had one minor accident (I reversed into a metal post at the end of a drive), causing only minor damage. During the tours I had the odd confrontation, usually due to people's misplaced suspicions, but on the whole I was met only with friendship and courtesy. One notable exception occurred during an early evening's exploration of the docks at Seaham, when a security officer gave me a dressing-down, notwithstanding his colleague having granted me permission to enter the area. Some notable events occurred during the tours, including the death of Diana, Princess of Wales, a total eclipse of the sun, a General Election and at least one FA Cup Final. Eventually, having driven more than 10,000 miles, on 8 June 2001, exactly five years to the day since leaving for Carlisle on that first morning, I drove the last mile through lanes to Joan Croft level crossing, the nearest accessible point to Shaftholme Junction, which had always been my intended goal and where I may have imparted something of the occasion to the young lady crossing-keeper, before leaving for home.

Throughout the project it was never my intention to seek to publish the work – indeed, it wouldn't have been half as much fun had that been the case. Not long after completion I did make enquiries about having a copy made until I reconsidered the other option of having the work published, which is where we are today. This book encompasses the first five tours undertaken between June 1996 and May 1997 and covers the area north and west of Newcastle-upon-Tyne to the Scottish Border; perhaps other books on the remaining tours will follow. Besides my gratitude to Silver Link I would like to thank Neville Stead for supplying all the 'past' photographs, David Pearce for placing his collection of photographs at my disposal, Cambridge University Library for supplying all the large-scale mapping, and Phyllis Bartlam for her encouragement and assistance with the typing.

Mike Griggs

BIBLIOGRAPHY

Biddle, Gordon and Nock, O. S. *The Railway Heritage of Britain*

Caplan, Neil *Border Country Branch Line Album*

Clinker, C. R. *Clinker's Register of Closed Passenger Stations and Goods Depots*

Cooke, R. A. and Hoole, K. *North Eastern Railway Historical Maps*

Gammell, C. J. *LNER Branch Lines*

Hoole, K. *A Regional History of the Railways of Great Britain, Vol 4, The North East*
Forgotten Railways, North East England
North Eastern Locomotive Sheds
North Eastern Branch Lines since 1925

Sewell, G. W. M. *The North British Railway in Northumberland*

Smith, Paul *The Handbook of British Railways Steam Motive Power Depots, Vol 4 Northern England and Scotland*

EPISODE 1

THE NEWCASTLE-CARLISLE LINE
AND BRANCHES

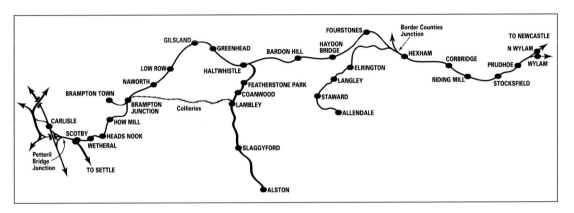

8 June 1996

The first tour to the Newcastle & Carlisle Railway took place early in June, with the weather predominantly sunny throughout. It was non-stop to **Carlisle**, where at 10.45am I stopped in a side road that led to the old railway cottages adjacent to the goods yard at Petteril Bridge.

Walking towards the city centre, I crossed the railway and came to a curious building, which I stupidly took to be the original N&CR London Road station! It was, in fact, a tram repair depot, now in use as a garage business. Down the side, a cobbled way led to what had once been a large engine shed and goods warehouse. The dual roundhouses existed as part of a factory, flanked on two

sides by more modern structures, which were also brick-built. **1*** The whole area was securely fenced off and difficult to photograph owing to road-transport vehicles parked outside. A small stone-built structure, possibly the shed offices, lay at the back of the yard.

The large goods warehouse, also brick-built, lay across the cobbled way and had a large administration block adjacent to London Road. At the far end, situated amongst the grass-covered sidings still present in the goods yard, was another small building with a pitched slated roof, now home to a flock of pigeons. **2** From London Road the N&C tracks led eastwards for almost a mile to the next bridge

---

* Numbers in bold within the text refer to specific photographs, which are also numbered accordingly

▲ 1 Roundhouse, Carlisle London Road

▼ 2 Carlisle London Road goods shed, looking west

▼ 3 LNWR carriage sheds and River Petteril, Upperby

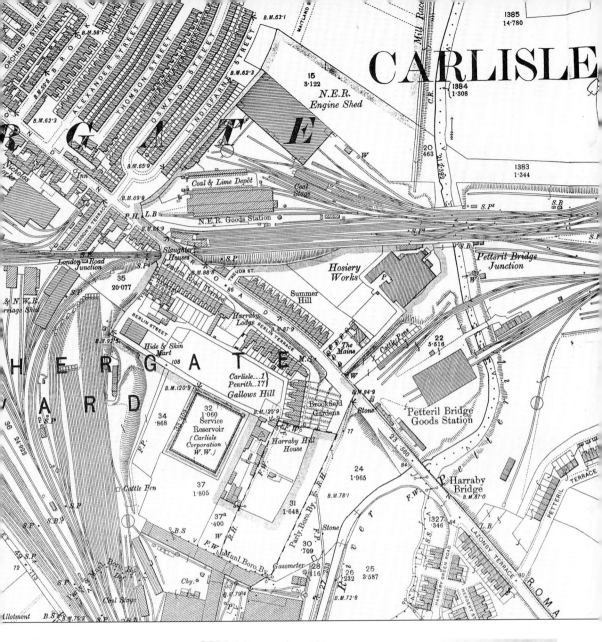

▲ Petteril Bridge Junction, Carlisle

▶ **4** The site of the small G&SWR shed at Petteril Bridge

where the site of the Midland Railway's roundhouse at Durranhill lay unused.

On the way back to Petteril Bridge I passed the entrance to Carlisle Upperby LNWR, shed and also an old brick-built stables or similar, probably of Midland Railway origin, below road level, just north of the river. On crossing the road, an old LNWR carriage shed with arched doorways lay on high ground south of the river, dominating the skyline. **3** The site of Carlisle Harraby, the small, short-lived G&SWR shed, tucked away in the extreme south-west end of the Midland Railway's yards, lay just south of the river. **4** After a preliminary examination of the shed site, which was now under a large area of concrete being part of a disused factory, I followed a footpath through an opening running parallel to, but below, London Road. Soon I was walking along the tree-lined banks of the river and into an area where the vegetation was enlivened by areas of golden whin interspersed with may-blossom. Two old sidings remained, and as I returned to the riverside a passing train, bound for Citadel station, crossed the river bridge.

Returning to civilisation I set course for the village of **Wetheral**, where I first compared the view of the station from the road bridge with that in some old photographs. I then walked on a footpath along the side of the cutting to the station. The station building and adjacent station house were well-kept, and, from the top of the footbridge (all footbridges on this

line are the originals), I looked eastward as a 'Sprinter' unit set off over the viaduct bound for Newcastle. **5** Only the site of the erstwhile signal box, perched high on the cutting side, could not be detected.

I returned and took the main road to **Brampton**, where I found the remains of the Town station at the rear of an old garage with an interesting collection of cars, mostly in a state of decay. The proprietor indicated that the old station building was now the bungalow immediately behind their premises, but it was not possible for me to intrude further due to an elderly lady knitting in the porch and watching my every move!

It was too hot to walk the long mile along the trackbed to the Junction station, so a few minutes later I had parked in a dead-end lane next to a country cottage at the station entrance. In the old goods yard were the remnants of a sawmill, while across the tracks the shell of a signal box remained next to the junction with the closed colliery line to Lambley. I walked at the back of the eastbound platform for a short distance along the 'Dandie Way', now a country footpath to Brampton (Town), and returned along the platform past a wooden waiting shelter, now without panelling or windows. **6**

The road east led to **Greenhead**, a hamlet of cottages and small railway hotel where I sampled a glass of Jennings's bitter while I briefly escaped the heat of the day. I was,

◄ **5** Wetheral station

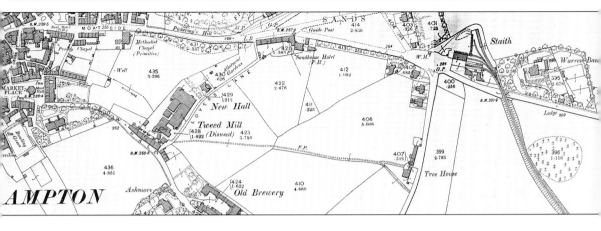

▲ Brampton Town station (right) and the town itself (left)

P. B. Booth

▲ ▶ **6** Brampton Junction, looking east on 5 June 1965, and in 1996

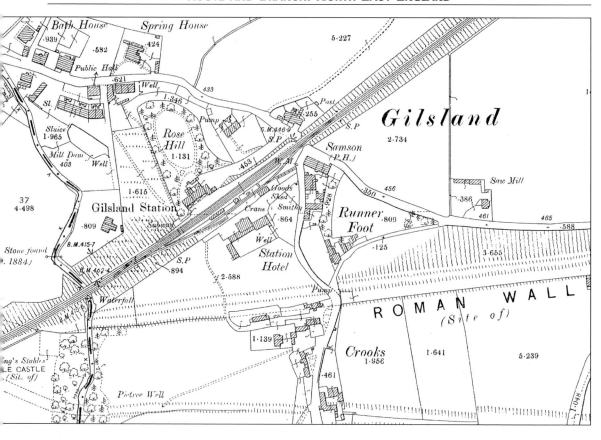

▲ Gilsland station, between Brampton Junction and Haltwhistle

however, impatient to continue and set off down the lane to the old station house, with a goods office and crane adjoining in the small goods yard area. **7** Chatting with the residents, I was very dubious when told that the (previously undiscovered) engine shed was, in fact, the building now being used as a garage store, and I was forbidden to photograph the pit inside due to the owner not wishing to receive an avalanche of visitors!

It was now mid-afternoon and I had moved on to **Haltwhistle**. The small town was quiet, with people enjoying the sunshine, as I crossed the road and walked along the station approach, noting that there were still a number of sidings in the old goods yard. **9** The approach widened into a turning space, where I examined the stone-built edifice supporting the large water tank, now a listed building. The

station buildings are also beautifully preserved, as is the wooden waiting shelter on the island platform. **8** Further sidings existed at the south-east end of the station together with a turntable, but these had been lifted and the area cleared. Returning along the platform past a long-disused water column, I found that nothing remained of the goods shed, though part of the back wall still stood. From the footbridge the view east, past the signal box to the viaduct over the River Tyne on the Alston branch, was bathed in sunshine. **10**

I left Haltwhistle, passing some unidentified bridge abutments leading northward from the main line, then came to **Haydon Bridge**, where I found the station down a quiet road. From the level crossing I walked along the platform, passing the rather plain station building, although a climbing plant on the gable end was in full bloom. **11** Across from the end of the platform were the remains of the goods yard, together with an interesting stone-built

▶ **7** Greenhead station, looking west on 7 June 1965, and in 1996

P. B. Booth

▼ **8** Haltwhistle station, looking east

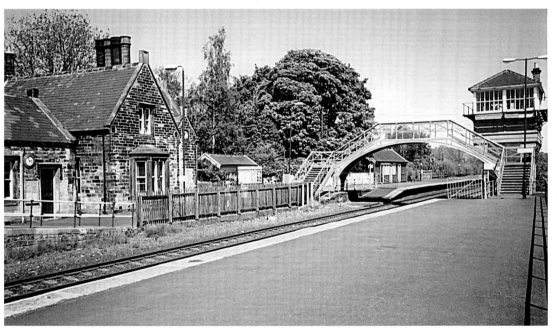

▲◀ **9** Haltwhistle station, looking west

▶ **10** Haltwhistle station, looking

bungalow, which may have had railway origins. It was here that I decided to get a closer look at the remains of the goods yard, so rather than risk direct entry off the platform end I returned and found the entrance marked by two stone pillars. It was a private road and led past a terrace of old cottages and on across some rough ground to a coal merchants' business, which has maintained much of the original character of the yard. **12**

▲ **11** Haydon Bridge station, looking east from the level crossing

▼ **12** Haydon Bridge, coal yard

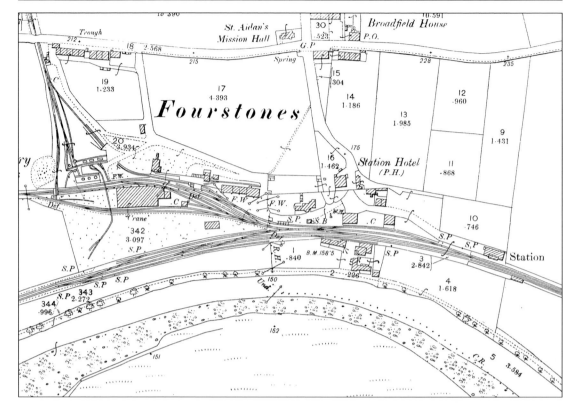

▲▼ Fourstones station, between Haydon Bridge and
Hexham, photographed on 9 April 1966

P. B. Booth

The afternoon remained sunny as I arrived at **Hexham** and, with somewhat diminished enthusiasm, made my way on foot towards the station, as I was parked some distance away. In the remains of the large goods yard was a neat stone-built goods shed, in private use but still in good original condition. The engine shed site alongside was unused, but between it and the still extant cattle docks were an array of civil engineering spares. Bordering the site was a terrace of old cottages and an old brick warehouse. The station was quite busy, as was the railway, with numerous service trains operating during the afternoon. **13** I climbed the old footbridge to view the goods yard and large elevated signal cabin spanning the tracks to the east. **14** Also of interest was the coal yard, with many of the old features lying undisturbed and flanked by a row of brick-arched stores beneath the ramped approach road. Driving through the small town I was pleased to arrive at my night's stay on the western fringe of the town.

After a brief shower I headed eastwards, stopping first at Corbridge station, where the

building is now an Indian restaurant. The heat of the day was diminishing as I came to **Riding Mill**, where the idyllic station building backed on to the platform. I drank a flask of coffee while seated on the platform listening to the evening bird chorus. A single-coach DMU came in and stopped before departing for Carlisle.

Continuing, I came to Stocksfield, where the station lay beside the main road. The goods yard was empty but, typically, a useful small tarmacked car park had been provided. Here the station house lay isolated from the station, surrounded by a large garden.

I then drove towards Prudhoe where, leaving the main road, I took a long side road through this large industrial village where the many rows of terraced houses, situated on the hillside overlooking the valley, were reminiscent of the county of Durham, with Newcastle just 12 miles away. Following a diversion, I drove down a steep hill that gradually narrowed and I became lost, eventually arriving in the village of Wylam, which was not on the itinerary! I resisted the temptation to stop at the station and passed over the Tyne and through the 'picture

▼ Hexham station

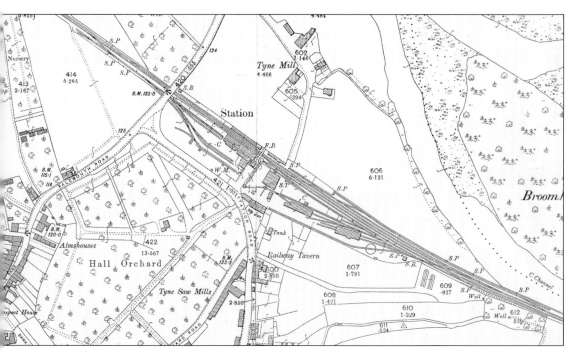

▲▼ **13** Hexham station, west end

▼ **14** Hexham station, looking east, with the shed site just past the end of the loading dock

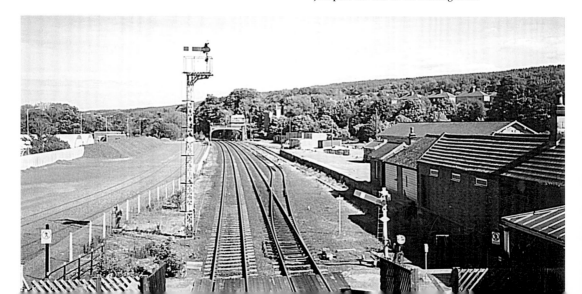

▲ Riding Mill station, with a Carlisle-Newcastle train passing

▼ Border Counties Junction, with Border Counties route to Reedsmouth north, Carlisle line north-west, and Allendale branch west

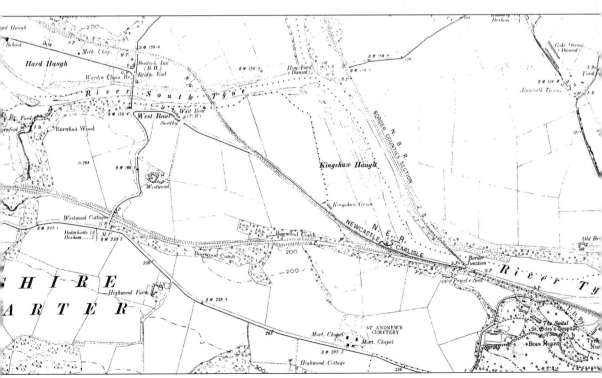

postcard' village, seeing George Stephenson's cottage before re-crossing the river to find Prudhoe station by a level crossing. I did not linger here longer than was necessary and after a walk along the platform I returned to the village of Corbridge, where I ate fish and chips from a small shop in the square.

Back at Hexham I found I was unable to reach 'Old Bridge End', near where the Border Counties Railway had crossed the River Tyne, due to road alterations, but after putting my car 'to bed' my landlady gave me clear directions how to get there on foot. The route lay over a golf course and down a rough track before crossing the railway. Walking west, beside the river, I came to Border Counties Junction, where the remains of the four bridge supports lay across the river, and the solitary house on the far side was the aforementioned 'Old Bridge End'. The scene was lit by the setting sun, but to photograph it meant a somewhat precarious scramble along the steep bank of the river.

The way ahead led to the Boat Inn about a mile and a half distant through narrow lanes that led across the river just upstream of the confluence of the North and South Tynes. After a glass of stout I left to walk the 3 miles back to Hexham. The way led up a steep hill to the main road, crossing an old bridge over the closed branch to Allendale. Pushing on I passed the golf course entrance and walked to

a Vaux hotel at the far end of town. Late in the evening I returned via some of the town's streets and retired to bed after a hearty supper.

9 June 1996

Next morning I woke late and after breakfast drove first to the Allendale branch, with its three intermediate stations. At Elrington, set amidst high upland pastures, the formation had blended in with its surroundings. Sheep grazed on its unpretentious single platform and the station house now echoed to the sound of bleating. Next was **Langley**, where the old station was set amongst woodland and was pleasantly landscaped, serving as the village Post Office. **15**

The line soon left the dense woodland and at **Staward** the old station waiting room, built to the traditional pattern, had re-opened as a tea room. The station house, also on the platform, was a private dwelling. **16** Continuing over the moors I came to Allendale, where the station site had become a small caravan park. Several buildings remained, however, including the station house. **17** The town itself was small but on a grand scale, its large square surrounded by grand country inns. Several roads led off and I left the village through farming country and, after descending to the Alston road, drove towards Haltwhistle over the moors. The sun

◀ **15** Langley station

16 Staward station, looking north with the last pick-up goods to Allendale on 20 November 1950, and looking south in 1996

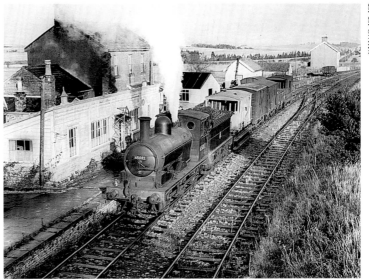

E. E. Smith

▼ Allendale station, with the same last-day pick-up goods

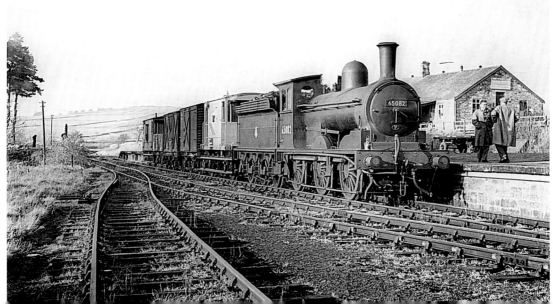

E. E. Smith

▲ 17 Allendale station, with its original wide platform

was strong and my arms had been quite badly burned during the previous day's driving! I passed a small mining company extracting surface coal before descending and crossing the Tyne into Haltwhistle. I then carried on to Greenhead, where I had been unable to photograph the front of the alleged engine shed the day before. This time a lane on the other side of the railway led to a spot from where I photographed the station area looking eastwards.

I left the village, climbing steeply out of the valley before slowly descending into the next. After driving up the valley for a short distance I crossed the shoulder of a hill to arrive at **Featherstone Park** station, the first stop out of

▼ 18 Featherstone Park station

▲▶ **19** Lambley station, looking north in the 1950s and in 1996

Haltwhistle on the Alston branch. Here only a short platform remained, and as the name suggests it was set in parkland. The railway track is now a long-distance footpath. **18**

I returned towards Greenhead, crossing the South Tyne before turning off to **Lambley**. Parking in the lane leading down to the village, I followed the footpath towards the station, which, due to the new owners' requirements, necessitated a lengthy detour under a viaduct before reaching the trackbed at the south end. The viaduct, not to be confused with the far longer structure over the South Tyne, had once carried a little-known mineral railway over the moors to Brampton

Junction. It rose high above the gorge and was partly scaffolded, with repair work well advanced. The station had not fared well, and the separate wooden waiting room was a ruin due to fire damage. **19**

Walking steeply out of the wooded defile I crossed a field with extensive views across to Coanwood station on the far side of the valley. As I drove on to Slaggyford I recalled a railtour to the line in the early 1970s, which had been a missed opportunity to see the line in its last months of operation. Once in the village I found that the station, on the western fringe, was occupied and had not been greatly altered, then drove through pleasant green

▲ **20** Alston station

◀ **21** Alston station, with a double-headed train arriving from Haltwhistle on 29 July 1952, and in its present narrow-gauge guise in 1996

meadows, with the South Tynedale Railway visible at intervals before arriving in **Alston**. **20** My last visit had been on a rainy afternoon 20 years earlier, and, as very often happens, the weather was just the opposite of my previous visit. The station itself had been well restored and would surely benefit from replacement of the overall roof and small lean-to engine shed. **21** An interesting narrow gauge engine brought a train across the level crossing at the platform end just as I arrived. The gates are operated from a rebuilt signal box, and give access to the car park adjacent to the station. Everywhere was clean and tidy, but on a previous visit, three years after the line closed, I can recall posters up at the windows of the disused building indicating that the railway had a future. Facing the station frontage the goods shed is in fair condition but in alternative use.

I left Alston and headed up on to the moors where a great number of motor cyclists had gathered at a hilltop café. The road descended in a series of hairpin bends, and here I stopped, lay on the roadside and admired the view, which easily encompassed the Lake District mountains, and over the Solway Firth to south-west Scotland. Somewhere in the valley was the Settle & Carlisle line, but it remained out of sight until I came to the village of Langwathby, where the beautifully preserved station building is now a restaurant. **22**

By the time I reached Penrith the afternoon had become cloudy. Following the Shed Directory, I parked in a lane on the west side of the station and continued on foot over some waste ground. Alas, the green fields had been sacrificed to the inevitable industrial estate, which backed on to the railway. After much deliberation I decided that any further exploration was unwise due to the possibility of setting off the alarm fixed to the building! All was not lost, however, as I returned to the station through the underpass and headed down the now much extended platform at the southern end of the station. The yard was empty but much of the track was still in situ, and just acxross the tracks was the unit that had identified the shed's position. **23** I resisted the temptation to cross a track from a little-used platform as a short-cut back to the car and instead retraced my steps, passing on the way one of those large noisy public houses that always seem to be open on a Sunday afternoon! This visit had been altogether more successful than my last, when, returning from Scotland about 20 years earlier with insufficient time, I had been unable to follow the directions in the Shed Directory.

I drove south along the A6 and soon turned left along a country road, passing under the

▼ **22** Langwathby station, Settle & Carlisle line

▲ **23** Penrith – the shed site

main line. A huddle of houses down a rough track on my left was the forgotten station of Clifton on the Kirkby Stephen to Penrith line. My arrival was greeted with some surprise, when askin if I was on a public road. Soon I was talking with the occupants of the other two buildings, who were returning with their dogs after a walk over the fields. All the main station buildings have survived; the station master's house and the down-side station

building have rear extensions, but the other building looks quite original externally. **24** I wandered around the goods yard through banks of weeds where the ramp of the coal drop siding survived, as did the small goods office and the weathered remains of a tiny goods shed. I left this North Eastern Railway outpost with the intention of resuming my wanderings at Riccarton Junction in the ensuing weeks.

▼ **24** Clifton station

Episode 2
Central Northumberland

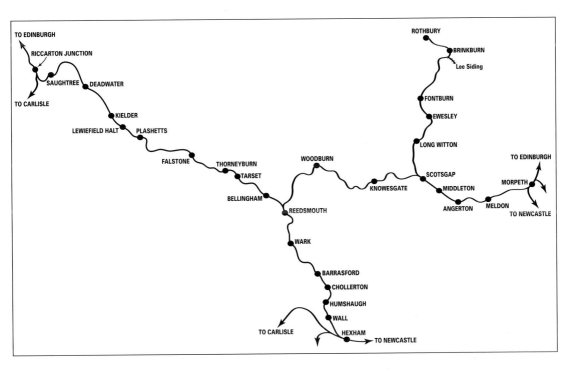

17 August 1996

After the previous weekend it had been my intention to continue with the exploration of the North British Railway lines in Northumberland; however, I had decided in the meantime to work from east to west rather than vice versa.

By 11.30am on 17 August I was clear of the Tyne Tunnel 'bottleneck' and, keeping clear of the worst of the Saturday morning queues, parked at Morpeth station. It was soon obvious that there was quite a lot to absorb, but, as planned, I did not stay longer than it took to consume two sandwiches (looking around at the same time of course) as I intended to return at a later date. The fuel gauge was edging towards the red as I headed south before

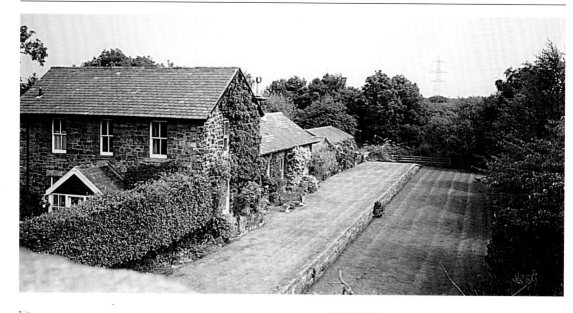

▲ **1** Meldon station, looking east

◀ **2** Angerton station, looking east

▼ **3** Middleton station, looking west; the station house is in the trees on the left

turning right down some very pleasant country roads. I soon came to **Meldon** station, set amidst open cornfields but surrounded by trees. The station, closed in 1952, looked well restored but the goods yard was totally overgrown and there was no possibility of further exploration. **1** I then journeyed west to **Angerton**, where the winding lane had crossed the railway at an unprotected crossing. The station on the east side was largely obscured by a high coniferous hedge, and again provided a pleasant country home. **2** The long-disused coal yard on the other side of the crossing lay in a clearing amongst trees. Driving on through open country, I came to **Middleton** where, just past the overbridge, I clambered up the embankment and found that the station platform was heavily overgrown, as was the short loading stage opposite. The adjoining station house was inhabited and, unlike Meldon and Angerton, there is a small village community nearby. **3**

I quickly drove to **Rothbury**, nearly 20 miles away, arriving at 1.20pm, and with some relief filled up with petrol. I spent some time assessing the station yard, which had been re-developed, and left soon after 2 o'clock, somewhat disappointed with my observations.

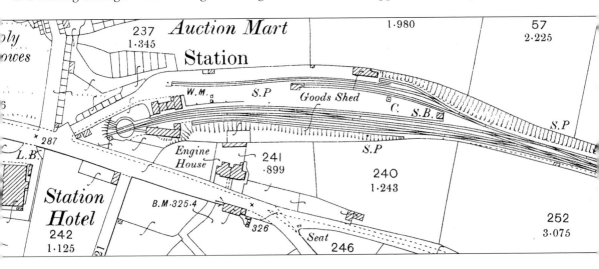

▲ Rothbury station

▶ Rothbury station, with an
   excursion from Newcastle

◀ Brinkburn station on 15 July 1952

▼ Lee Siding and Lee Colliery

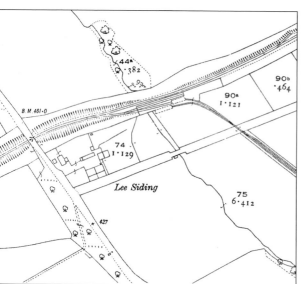

The switchback road continued for 2 miles until a left turn took me to Lee Siding, between Brinkburn and Fontburn, where there was once a connection with a short mineral railway to a nearby colliery – the formation could clearly be seen on the side of a hill to the east. I had to give up going to Brinkburn station, partly due to lack of time, but also as I had inadvertently left the OS map of this area at home.

Driving south, I stopped just short of the bridge where the Fontburn siding used to serve a colliery about a mile to the south-east.

All traces of this had long faded into the landscape, but the trackbed continued to Fontburn, which could only be reached (legally) by following the trackbed north from Ewesley, but again I could not risk deviating here as very often these incursions can take longer than expected! The short curved platform at **Ewesley** and the station house still lingered on **4**, and from there the line continued eastwards, immediately crossing the Rothbury road where the bridge abutments were still in place. It then made a semi-circle,

▲ **4** Ewesley station house, with the trackbed on the right

▼ **5** Long Witton station, only just demolished; there is a bridge under the road in the trees

crossing the road about 2 miles to the south at **Long Witton**, where the small ruinous station building had only recently been removed, but the base could easily be seen. **5** I stopped for some food here and, reflecting on progress so far, concluded that as usual a compromise had had to be reached and it was inevitable that some sites would remain unseen.

Soon time was on my side as I was not detained long at **Scotsgap Junction**, where the Northumberland Central Railway (the Rothbury branch) left the Wansbeck Valley line. The small village community comprised a caravan park, a couple of garage premises and a number of agricultural businesses within the station yard. The station was hemmed in by more mundane structures, but the station house was pleasantly situated on the west side. **6** The Rothbury branch junction to the west could just be seen from the road bridge, which provided a good vantage point for the site generally. **7**

I drove west on a dull but sometimes bright afternoon as the fields turned to moorland. Soon the line crossed over the road and ran through some lonely terrain to the hamlet of **Knowesgate**. Access here was not easy, and I first walked along an unsurfaced track beside a stone building I took to be the station, but in doing so I disturbed two dogs and got the usual response! **8**

▲◀ **6** Scotsgap station, with a pick-up goods from Blyth to Rothbury, and in 1996

◀ **7** Bridge at Scotsgap, looking west

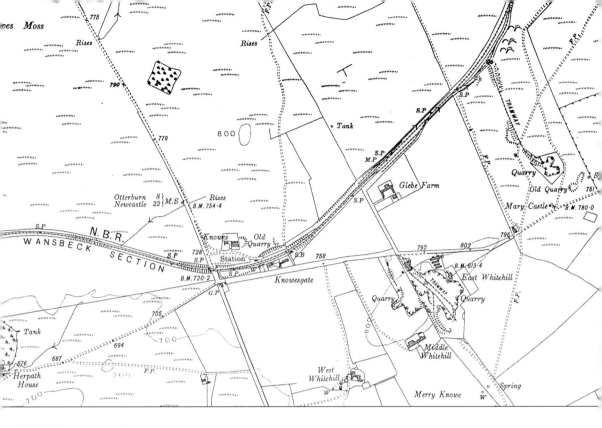

▲▼ 8 Knowesgate station

Taking a less than satisfactory photograph due to the dull conditions, I quickly returned and drove on towards Woodburn. On the way I passed the Summit Cottages some distance away down a side road, standing alone amongst the moors and marking the point where the line began to fall towards Reedsmouth.

Soon I turned right on to the A68 (the main road to Scotland) and within a mile came to **Woodburn** station on a steep hill to the south of the village. There, to the east of the bridge, the station appeared 'railway-like', having not been altered to any extent. **9** Further on, round the curve, several modern houses had been built on or near the railway.

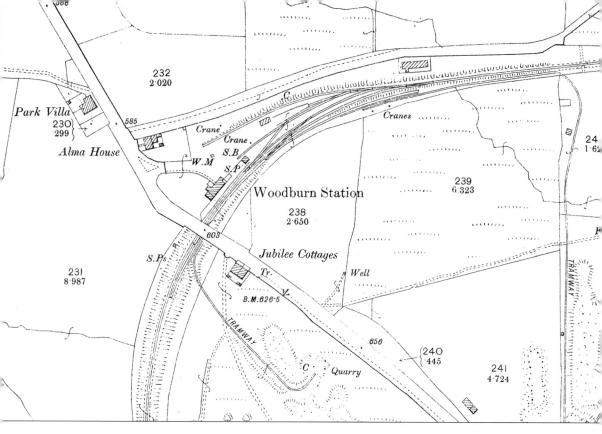

Having explored the Wansbeck Valley, I drove south towards Hexham to begin exploration of the Border Counties Railway where I had left off at Border Counties viaduct some ten weeks before. I parked first at Acomb, a village about a mile north-west of the junction, which once had a connection with the railway, serving a coal mine on the north side of the village. As it was now about 5 o'clock I finished my sandwiches before continuing further, while a large boxer dog, just over the fence, went through the motions of barking without sounding very convincing. Returning north towards the small village of **Wall**, I turned down a steep track towards the old station. There I was given a conducted

▶ **10** Wall station, rebuilt but with the original signal box

▼ **11** Humshaugh station

tour, particularly of the signal box, which was almost original externally and was being converted into living accommodation, while the station building had been rebuilt by an enthusiast but, understandably, not to the original design. **10** After quite a long conversation I left and decided to head straight for the inn at Humshaugh, where I was to spend the night.

Within half an hour I was back on the road, reasonably refreshed, and drove to **Humshaugh** station, renamed from Chollerford in 1919, only a short drive away on the far bank of the North Tyne. Looking more like a fine country house, the station and small goods shed are

now in far better condition than during the last years of operation of the railway. **11** The evening was cool but sunny as I turned down Cocklaw Lane and parked by some bridge abutments intending to make up for not having made time to locate the many mineral extraction systems connected with the railway. I proceeded along an embankment with far-reaching views towards the river while, to the left, the hillside rose steeply. After a short distance I came to the remains of two lime kilns and a loading dock, and climbing to the top found the view westward extended for several miles; I was also surprised to find some old rusty rails remaining over the top of

▲◄ **12** Cocklaw Sidings, and the view from the top of the lime kilns, with rails still in situ

the kilns. **12** I gazed uphill towards Cocklaw quarries and tried to imagine the various systems that, over the years, had carried limestone down the 1 in 7 incline.

I then drove on to Chollerton, passing under a graceful stone viaduct, and parked next to several old stone houses, any of which could have been the station. I was aware of being observed by a lady in the largest house, so I made a pretence of being interested in the church opposite, and only at the last second walked down the side of an old cottage undergoing some restoration. I was surprised to find the overgrown

platform and a small green corrugated iron shelter still in situ, but to the north of where I was standing.

I continued the short distance to **Barrasford** and found the station building at the far end of a road leading eastward from the main road; the pleasantly original single station building took up most of the platform length. **13**

On the way from Chollerton I had paused to photograph the line in the distance across fields of corn but now, as food came to mind, I continued for several miles to **Wark**, the only settlement in the area where some might be

▶ **13** Barrasford station

▼ **14** Wark station, looking south

available. Some distance before the village I turned right up a winding lane to find the remotely situated station. **14**

Having recorded the scene, I drove back down the hill, crossing the North Tyne on a girder bridge, and entered Wark, a typical moorland village. It had three pubs and I was soon in the Black Bull, where, after a well-earned pint, I decided that I fancied fish and chips, which meant driving 12 miles back to Hexham. I was pleased to return to what, in comparison, seemed a very big town, and ate in the quiet Abbey grounds, which were open to the public. At about 8.30pm I drove back towards Humshaugh and my hotel, but was pleased to stop at the commendable inn in Wall, where I again made myself comfortable!

18 August 1996

It was a cool but sunny morning as I drove through lanes to **Reedsmouth**. A previous visit in 1976 had for some reason revealed almost nothing of the railways, but after turning down a narrow road towards the mill (and also, as it happens, to Reedsmouth House) I parked under some sycamore trees and cheerfully made and ate a cheese sandwich. This consumed, I set off on foot along a farm track and, arriving at the Border Counties line, came across the quite large engine shed. Plenty of original brickwork was visible, but the building was heavily clad, both the roof and sides, in asbestos sheets. **15** On one side lay a veritable mountain of farm manure, while cattle crowded around its entrance. Braving swarms of flies, I looked at the north end of the building before taking the footpath that led to the Border Counties platforms and the signal box. The whole area was clean and tidy, but the one remaining station building and rendered signal cabin were all that remained. **16** Most of the site was covered by luxuriant meadow grass as I photographed the junction and noted the wider formation of the Wansbeck Valley route heading under the first bridge towards Woodburn. I left feeling quite pleased, as I had expected access to be more difficult.

▲ **15** Engine shed, Reedsmouth

◀ Reedsmouth station in 1952, with the pick-up goods bound for Riccarton Junction behind 'D30' 'Scott' 4-4-0 No 62422 *Caleb Balderstone*

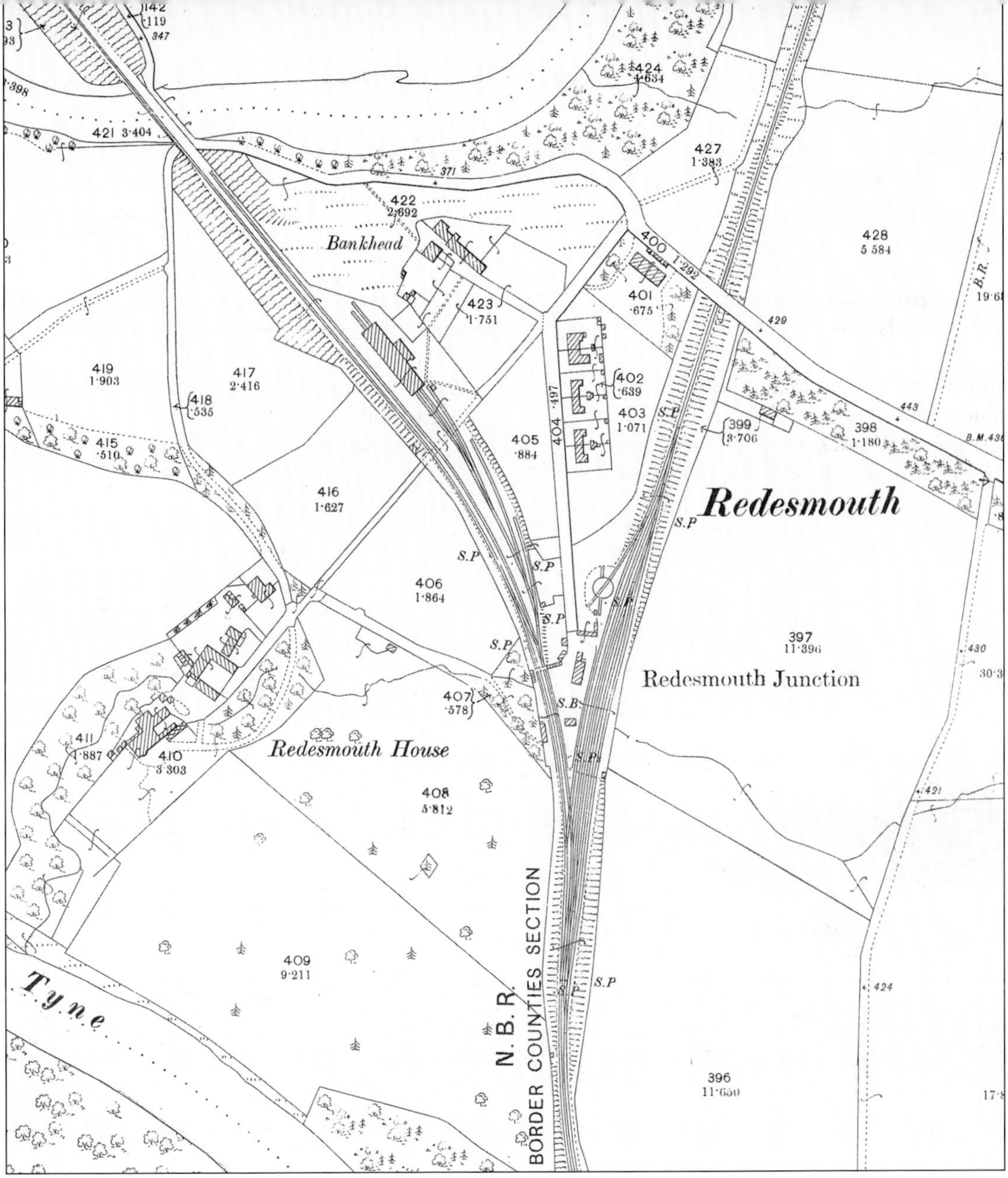
Bankhead
Redesmouth
Redesmouth Junction
Redesmouth House
Tyne
N.B.R.
BORDER COUNTIES SECTION

▲ Reedsmouth Junction

▼ **16** Reedsmouth station, looking north

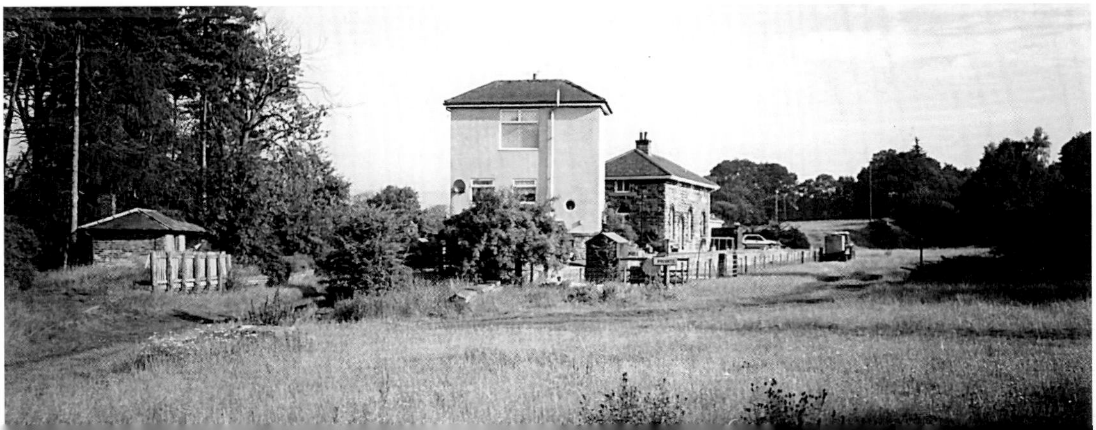

▲◀ **17** Bellingham station and signal box, and the station building and platform in 1996

▶ Footbridge at Riding Wood west of Bellingham

▲ Bellingham and its station

Continuing west, I came to **Bellingham**, after following the bare trackbed, which ran parallel to the road. I found the station site next to a council yard, chain-link fencing making it awkward but not impossible to record the scene. **17** As I continued past a long row of terraced cottages standing well above the railway, it was obvious that the exertions of the previous day had taken their toll on my resources! I edged down a bank over some waste ground and pushed through some shrubbery to an old rusting fence, which revealed a little more detail of the site. Back at the main road, I left the township and headed west, away from this last pocket of civilisation.

After about a mile and a half I came to the railway again, where a well-preserved footbridge crossed the formation at Riding Wood. I took a photograph and drove to the road bridge just west of Tarset station. I was obliged to obtain a closer view than from the

bridge, so I walked along a surfaced track to the house nearly 200 yards away. As I mooched around I was pleased to see a couple of cats lying contentedly in the garden. I returned, hoping that I had not given any alarm to the residents in this lonely situation.

Leaving the main road I took a gated road towards Thorneyburn; the line follows this road quite closely as far as Falstone. The first obstacle was a herd of cows, which, judging by the road surface, was where they spent much of the day; I was relieved not to have injured any as I had literally to force my way past. The road passed through grassy meadows and soon came to **Thorneyburn** station, where the crossing-keeper's cottage is the only human habitation for several miles. **18**

I then continued towards Falstone, with fascinating views of the railway; the condition of the formation, even considering the terrain, made it appear that the line had only recently been closed, as most of the culverts, bridges and permanent-way huts were still there and in

◀ **18** The crossing-keeper's cottage at Thorneyburn station from near the level crossing

▼ **19** Falstone station, looking east

good condition. I passed through about three more gates before gradually the road became wider and the village of Falstone came into view, down the hillside to my left. I crossed a railway bridge and came to **Falstone** station, a large impressive building together with a space that was once the goods yard, which afforded an interesting view of the village. **19**

From here the railway entered a roadless tract of country and followed the North Tyne river to the Plashetts area some 6 miles away. The road, leaving the railway, crosses the valley and joins the 'main' road to the west, where I turned right. As the road broadened, Kielder Reservoir, built about 20 years earlier, came into view. There were boat trips to Plashetts where, although the station area is under water, the remains of a connection to the defunct colliery (at a higher level) could still be seen.

I continued towards Kielder and turned down a side road where I stopped in a clearing among fir trees that had been laid out as a picnic area. After 'lunch had been served', I walked the short distance to Kielder Viaduct, the largest structure on the line, and found that it had been restored. **20** I scrambled up the bank without too much trouble and crossed to the other end, noting the unusual castellated finish to the stonework. I would like to have continued to Lewiefield, just over a mile from Plashetts, where the station area is just

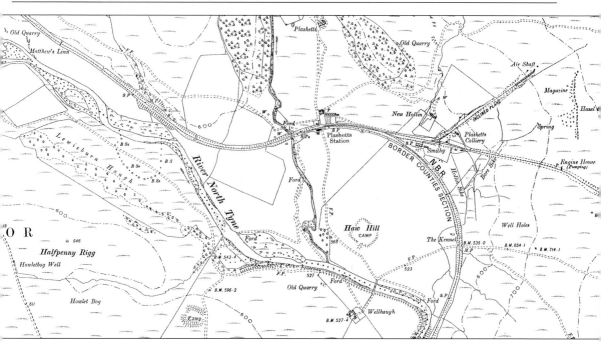

▲▼ Plashetts station, looking east, now beneath Kielder Reservoir

▲▼ **20** Kielder Viaduct across the North Tyne, and the
trackbed looking west

above the high-water mark, but instead I
returned and captured the view of the viaduct,
with the North Tyne flowing below.

Returning to the main road I found **Kielder**
station next door to a garage. The lady who
lived in the station building kindly removed
the washing from the back garden so I could
take a photograph. **21** I left Kielder, a
scattered settlement within the forest, and
drove through a mixture of moorland and
forest until the lonely station at **Deadwater**
came into view on the left, about a hundred
yards from the road. **22** Just to the west were

two old lime kilns with a graded bank to the
rear indicating a connection with a quarry in
the hills. As I had Riccarton foremost in my
mind, I did not delay and drove several more
miles through a pass in the hills, emerging at a
farm, two houses and a church which made
up the hamlet (sorry, township, as this is
Scotland) of Saughtree. At the T-junction I
turned right, and after about a mile **Saughtree**
station came into view on a hillside to my left.
I set out on foot and after a 5-minute walk
came to the delightfully isolated station with
tracks and some pointwork laid between the

▶ **21** Kielder station, from the road and from the platform side, looking north-west

▼ **22** Deadwater station in its remote setting

platforms. **23** There had been a possibility that I would set off for Riccarton Junction from here, but I thought my car would be safer back at the township, so I returned and prepared for the walk ahead, which I thought would take about 2 hours.

As there is no law of trespass in Scotland, I climbed over the nearest gate and set off uphill. After much exertion I came to easier ground and soon crossed the trackbed and continued to the hilltop. What a catastrophe – my intended route had been obliterated by a long swathe of pine woods heading downhill towards the Border Counties line about three-

◀ **23** Saughtree station, looking towards Riccarton Junction

▼ Riccarton Junction

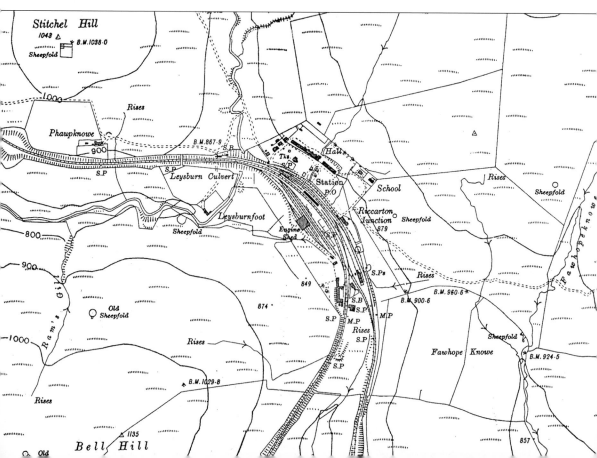

quarters of a mile away. All was not lost, however, as about half a mile away there was a fire-break in the woods. After some scrambling, I fought my way through grass 3 feet high to reach the top. It was an easy descent and below was the Border Counties line and, across the valley, running through pine woods, was the Waverley Route. As the tracks converged at **Riccarton Junction** the whole area seemed to be covered by rose-bay willow-herb, and to the east was a green slope with pockets of rhododendron and well-grown trees. The only building occupied was formerly the school, and a girl sitting on the front step watched my progress. I walked the whole length of the ruined platform, shorn of hardstanding and with some broken concrete slabs forming the walls still clinging to the edges. **24** The ruins of a row of cottages set

among a wood of sycamores were just visible through the trees. The only other structures remaining were a brick chimney (not worthy of Mr Dibnah!) and a small brick shed of unidentifiable origin.

The afternoon was warm and sunny as I regretfully started the walk back, the trackbed curving away from the Waverley Route through a pleasantly wooded cutting. Soon it crossed the valley on a very high embankment that I had seen from the hilltop soon after the start of the walk. A little further on I had to climb the cutting sides as a herd of cows came into view around the corner. In only a short time I was walking down the stony track back to the main road, and at about 3.00pm I started the journey southwards, broken only at the first shop, in a little village, where I bought an invaluable bottle of pop!

▲▼ **24** Riccarton Junction station, looking south towards the junction, and the site in 1996, with the ruined terrace of cottages in the trees on the right

Episode 3
North Northumberland

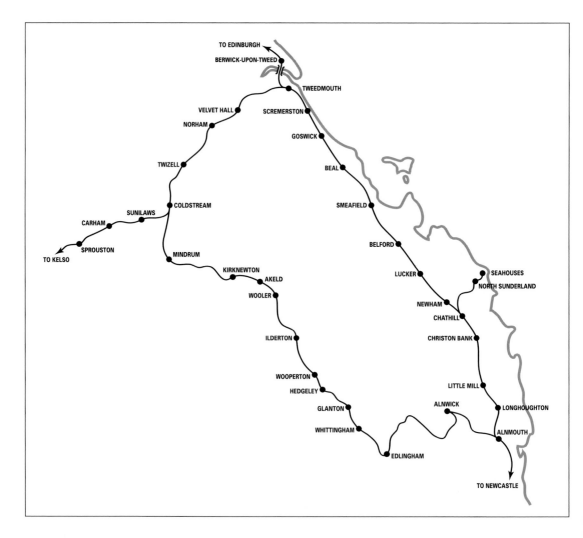

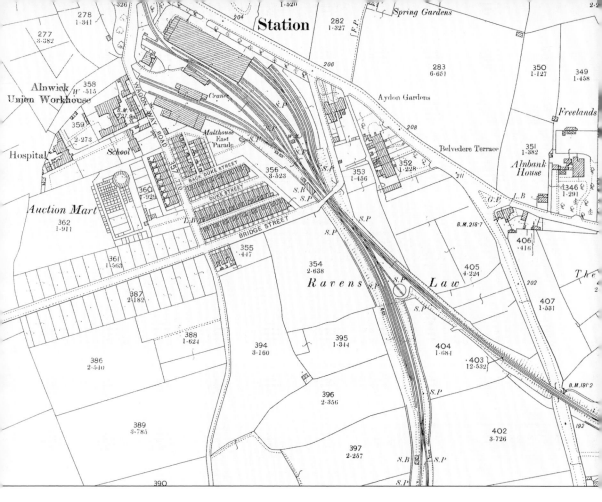

14 September 1996

▲ Alnwick station

The weather had been kind, and with good weather forecast the long non-stop grind up to Newcastle was over without too much hassle. By 11.30am I had parked in **Alnwick** below the green bank on which the lovely old station stood. It was warm and sunny as I entered the old goods yard, trying to summon up a degree of interest as I passed several business units, concealing the station on the west side. **1** As I came to the end it was clear that much landscaping had taken place at the front of the station building, which lay adjacent to the main road. I continued along the eastern wall, which was still in its original condition apart from one window that had been 'stretched' to form a doorway, accessed via a flight of steps well constructed in matching stone. I entered the building to find a well established second-hand-book business.

The atmosphere was akin to that of an old station waiting room, with dim lighting and varnished fittings, while the smell of old books hung in the air. I emerged into bright sunlight and crossed the station forecourt, little altered, I felt, since closure.

During my futile efforts to photograph the station frontage I had become increasingly doubtful as to the condition of my camera battery, which resulted in a pleasant walk through the small stone-built high street to obtain a replacement. After a frustrating wait to get served and only a slightly shorter one to find the battery compartment in my camera, I returned and drove west, soon taking a short break for a picnic on a grassy bank by the roadside. Another mile brought me to **Edlingham**, where I stopped at the end of the station drive. The view north and west was

▲◀ **1** Alnwick station, a general
view on 11 June 1957 and the
station site in 1996

◀**2** Edlingham station

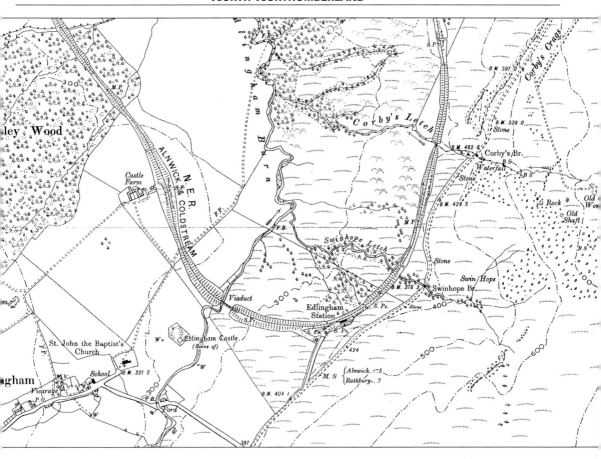

▲ Edlingham station

extensive and very clear, with rolling hills and, to the north, some higher tops, while just across the valley was the scattered settlement of Edlingham and the picturesque ruin of an old castle. **2**

Below the hillside the trackbed turned from west to north as it crossed the valley on a curving single-track viaduct. Some distance down the drive was the station house, which I did not approach, nor was there any easy way of gaining the trackbed without climbing over some barbed-wire fences. I had to assume that the station itself, built just below the station house, had been demolished, as I felt that it would have just been visible from the roadside.

I continued north, keeping to the main road that closely followed the line as far as Kirknewton. Quite soon I came to **Whittingham** station, about a mile from the

village, and first viewed the site from the overbridge to the south before entering the goods yard, where the goods office and the remains of coal drops were along the edge of the yard. **3** I talked with the people in the station house, who were cleaning their car, and asked if I could proceed further. With their approval I circled the goods shed, which was in a good state of repair, and noted that the station building on the island platform, still with metal canopy attached, was in sound (but unrestored) condition. A row of stone-built railway cottages adjacent to the road bridge were very well kept.

I left Whittingham, driving northward, and after a few minutes turned east down a side road with **Glanton** station visible across the fields. Stopping at the end of the station drive, I walked up to the station and again thought it prudent to ask permission before photographing the station buildings. **4**

◄**3** Whittingham station, looking
north circa 1952, and the station
and goods yard sites, also looking
north, in 1996 (note the coal drop
remains on the extreme left)

▶**4** Glanton station, and the site
looking north

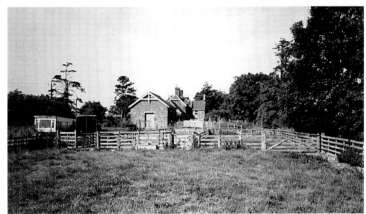

▼**5** Hedgeley station

▲ **6** Wooperton station

▲◄ **7** Ilderton station, looking north with a parcels train leaving, and in 1996, now a restaurant

With many more sites to visit, I was relieved that things had been straightforward so far.

The road north left the wide fertile vale and, as the hills closed in, the road joined the railway for a short distance before entering the pleasant village of Powburn, where **Hedgeley** station, a stone's-throw to the north, was named after the nearby Hall. Here I turned right and came to the site of a level crossing, while just to the north the formation soon crossed the River Beamish, where only the fine stone abutments remained. On impulse I entered a small fir wood and after some ducking and scrambling managed to catch sight of the station building. I then went in search of the front entrance, passing an old chap in a cottage garden who was somewhat taken aback at seeing me emerge from the wood! I had failed to notice the front of the station on arrival, due to the approaching road junction, but the 'generously proportioned' property and spacious grounds stood openly beside Hedgeley services, with its petrol and eating facilities. I was able to examine the building more closely by walking past the café and along a short service road that led down the entrance drive of the station back to the main road. **5**

The pleasant sunny afternoon was showing no signs of rushing by, so at the next station, **Wooperton**, I stopped and made coffee while looking at the station from the road bridge on the north side. Another large residence, with a substantial wood-cutting business on the site of the goods yard, it was out of all proportion to the tiny settlement it served. **6**

The pleasing Border countryside was a joy to drive through, with little traffic on the roads. **Ilderton** station, the first on the west side of the road, was now a beautifully restored restaurant set in landscaped grounds. A short length of track had been re-laid and an old restored coach stood in the platform next to the wooden waiting room, now used as a conservatory. **7**

Just before **Wooler**, the largest town on the line, the trackbed again dived under the road to pass the small town on its eastern flank. Rounding a bend, a large stone-built goods shed with surrounding wall suddenly appeared as I was about to try and find the station. **8** Pulling in, I set off on foot along a rough road before squeezing through a fence to take an unofficial short-cut used by locals over the years to get to the station. The large building had been converted into several dwellings, the long grandiose frontage being very well kept. **9**

The way north, regrettably, missed the town centre as I drove again into the 'wilds', stopping first at **Akeld**, now a beautifully kept house, with weighbridge and goods shed also in pristine condition. **10** I returned for a short distance towards Wooler before turning westward on a secondary road, passing through the village of **Kirknewton** and halting at the small station building of the same name built right on the roadside. Nearby was a rough track, which I followed to get a glimpse

▶ **8** Wooler goods shed

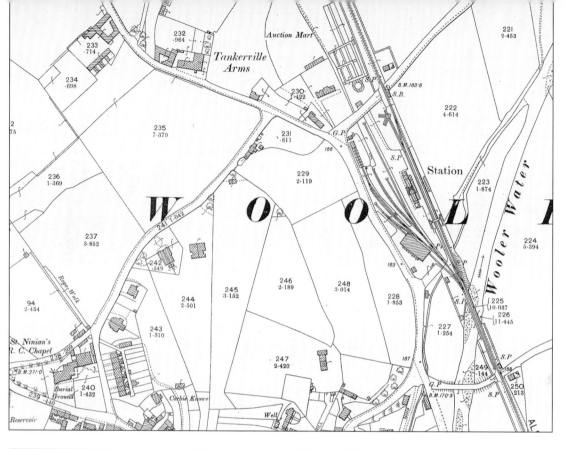

▲ Wooler station

◀**9** Wooler station

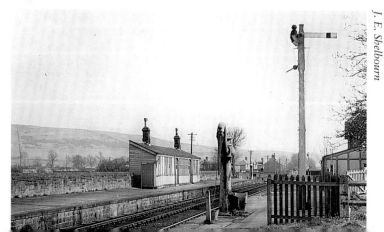

◀ Wooler station on 14 April 1952

▲ **10** Akeld station

▼ **11** Kirknewton station

▼ **12** Mindrum goods shed

of the rear of the building. I returned to the car and, walking some distance past the station and through a couple of field gates, I was able to get quite a good shot with the hills in the background. **11**

I pressed on towards **Mindrum** and soon realised that I was driving along the wrong side of the valley. Only a short distance back, however, I took a side road crossing an old tumbledown bridge to a T-junction where an old signpost proclaimed 'Mindrum station ½ mile' (although it had been closed for more than 30 years). The station, situated in a lane miles from anywhere, was another large residence with a stone-built goods shed in the grounds. Alongside, a small green-painted church, built of corrugated iron, right on the road, boasted a solitary gravestone round the back, and from here I was able to get a reasonable view of the goods shed. **12**

It was still only 4.20pm and time was not a problem for once. Therefore, instead of making straight for Coldstream, where the junction with the Berwick-Kelso line, to the south of the station at Cornhill-on-Tweed, marked the end of the route I had been following, I took the Kelso road and, making a right turn, descended steeply towards flatter country and the village of Sprouston.

I had first visited this small village, where the North Eastern and North British railways made an 'end on' junction, just over 20 years

earlier, but my memories did not concur with this visit. **Sprouston** station had then been isolated and in a ruinous state, but the whole area was now a small housing estate with the much extended station being the 'Manor House'. **13** Two boys were playing as I surveyed the station from the 'track' side. After much conjecture I walked eastward, passing some back gardens in search of the old level crossing, which I found on reaching the lane. Passing the 'well matured' trackbed on my right, I talked with a man busily reclaiming a weed-ridden verge, who obviously lived in the large bungalow built on the site of the small engine shed, which closed in 1916, just to the east of the station.

After quite a conversation I recorded the shed site on film before leaving for **Carham**, two stops out of Coldstream. I drove through lanes, searching the fields for a sign of the line, until, rounding a tight left-hand bend in the little-known settlement of Nottylees, I came to a short flat stretch of road halfway down a hill, clearly marking the site of a level crossing. Here I paused for refreshment as I tried to find an interesting view of the staggered platforms on either side of the road to take a photograph. Three plum trees, heavily laden with ripe fruit, grew by the end of the eastbound platform, but after looking at the pile of food in the boot I left them undisturbed! **14**

◀ **13** Sprouston. The large bungalow on the left is the site of the engine shed. The wall is a loading dock, which extended from the goods shed. The station is out of the picture to the left.

▲ **14** Carham station, showing one of the staggered platforms and the heavily laden plum trees

I drove on and, after taking the main road, drove through Carham village to the next village, where I turned right and followed a switchback road to the tiny hamlet of **Sunilaws,** which was in effect a short row of terraced houses and the station. As I got out of the car a group of bystanders stood aghast as I mounted the bank opposite the station to take a photograph of the small unpretentious building with its ex-NER wall clock still intact on a wall near the road. **15** Here again the platforms were staggered, and in the road at the site of the level crossing the old rails remained. I returned to the car and sped away to Wark, the village on the main road. I then continued to Cornhill-on-Tweed, on the English bank of the river, passing the junction of the Alnwick line some way to the east. Unfortunately Coldstream station area was now a new estate, although several older houses existed on the periphery. The station itself would have occupied the back gardens of some of the properties, but with no clear possibility of probing further I left and crossed the Tweed into Scotland at Coldstream.

▶ **15** Sunilaws station

I was soon ensconced in a small guest house in the centre of the town. About 2 hours later I enjoyed a takeaway on a grassy area by a stream that flowed into the Tweed. Afterwards I followed the stream to its confluence and, keeping to the riverside, passed a small camping field with a solitary tent near the water's edge. Here the river curved sharply beneath sheer walls of rock, rising perhaps 80 feet above the water, with several cottages on the skyline looking quite impregnable. With the light fading I continued along a walkway that gradually rose to the top of the cliff, surprisingly without a handrail or any protection against the sheer drop into the river. I returned along the main street and later, as the town could be walked from one end to the other in 5 minutes, walked backwards and forwards to seek out the most promising ale houses. My return at 11.20pm through the quiet streets left me feeling as I had in the morning – 'as fresh as a daisy'!

15 September 1996

The following day dawned bright, and after an early breakfast I set off towards Berwick-upon-Tweed. I had re-affirmed my original intention of not trying to visit every site of any interest, so I had intended to miss out Twizell due to lack of road access, and also not to visit every station site between Berwick and Alnmouth, my last call of the day. Setting off from Coldstream, I crossed the old stone bridge into Cornhill-on-Tweed and, driving on quiet roads, soon came to a road junction that I sensed would take me towards Twizell station. With no road showing on my map it came as a surprise, but unlike the East Coast Main Line sites, which could still be seen from the train, I was loth to miss this station.

The road towards **Twizell**, possibly opened up after the demise of the railway, ended by a couple of smallholdings, but a pot-holed way continued for perhaps 200 yards to the railway. The station house, on the edge of woodland, was still occupied and lay near the banks of the Tweed. One of the two staggered platforms remained, although it was so well

hidden that I had walked 30 yards alongside before seeing it.

I returned to the main road and soon turned left again into the same tract of country I had just left. In a mile I came to **Norham** station quite near the village, which, had I been aware of it, I would have taken the time to drive through it. The station and goods yard housed a large museum of railway artefacts and, although it was closed, I was fascinated in particular by the stone buildings in the goods yard, which begged closer inspection. **16** The station buildings could not be properly appreciated from the gate where I was standing, as the railway here was on an embankment.

Once again I returned to the main road to Berwick and soon came to **Velvet Hall** station, with the hall itself, looking more like an old farmhouse, on the opposite side of the road. There were no obvious remains of the railway apart from the large station building set well back from the road. **17**

I continued to **Berwick-upon-Tweed** and, after crossing the river, was able to park quite close to the station. It was still only 9 o'clock, and apart from a lad pointing the walls of an old inn close by, the town had yet to waken on this cool Sunday morning. After parking I made for the bridge to the north of the station, from where the engine shed site might be identified. Sure enough, a flat semi-circular area about 200 yards to the north with the correct background, as seen in an old photograph, made identification easy.

I then followed a tree-lined avenue on the east side of the line, from where I looked down on the railway across to the shed site. Next I had an obligatory look around the station, where all traffic now leaves from the island platform, accessed by a footbridge that was under restoration. **18** An HST, stabled to the north of the bridge, suddenly burst into life and slowly pulled into the station, which, apart from myself, appeared to be deserted. After the driver had changed ends the train headed off north again, and as I returned across the footbridge a southbound train sped through the station and across the Royal Border Bridge. **19**

▶ **16** Norham station

▶ **17** Velvet Hall station, looking north; the railway runs east to west parallel to the road

▼ **18** Berwick-upon-Tweed station frontage

19 Berwick-upon-Tweed station, with a southbound passenger train on 31 February 1964, and an HST passing through and heading for the Royal Border Bridge in 1996

◄ Berwick-upon-Tweed station, with a northbound passenger leaving on 13 August 1960

► Berwick-upon-Tweed, the Royal Border Bridge across the River Tweed, and Tweedmouth, showing the junction for the Coldstream line

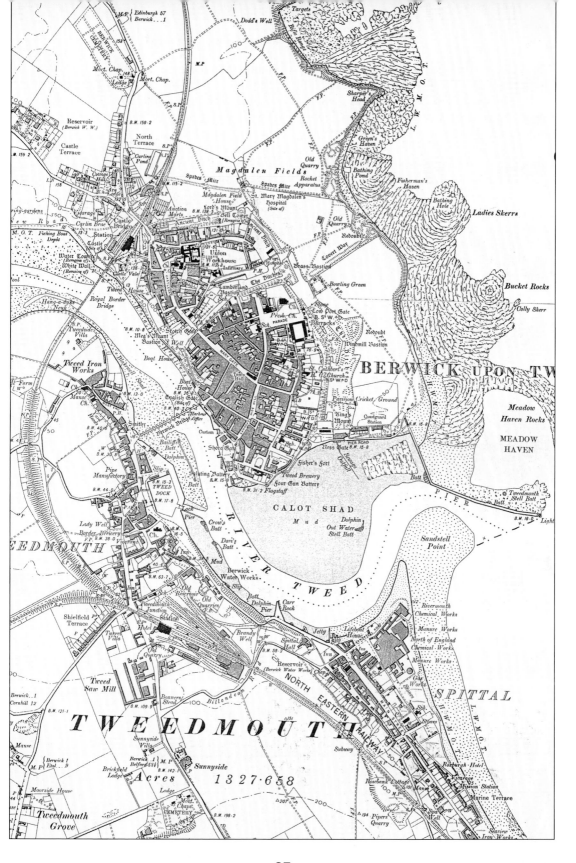

South of the bridge the East Coast Main Line swings eastward towards the coast, and soon I was heading for the better-known engine shed site at **Tweedmouth**, which had only closed in 1966. Finding the site of Tweedmouth station was not easy – only after going backwards and forwards many times, and after finding the engine shed, did the station site, just to the east of the road bridge across the old A1, become apparent. As my first attempts to find the station had been unsuccessful, I took a calculated guess and went in search of the engine shed. Taking a right-hand turn, the road rose to

higher ground, where I pulled in to assess the situation. From there, all was revealed: I had a clear view of the line right back to Berwick station. The shed, which was now part of a builders' merchants, backed on to a nearby road and had suffered the indignation of the paint brush. **20** The whole of the coastline and estuary of the Tweed lay before me, and the sight of the town of Berwick across the river was very interesting. Before leaving I drove into a small council estate that bordered the shed site and offered a view across the yard between the station and shed.

▲▼ **20** A distant view of Berwick and the Royal Border Bridge, with Tweedmouth engine shed the brightly painted building in the middle distance, also pictured circa 1938

P. B. Booth

▲ Tweedmouth station, looking south

I drove southward with the intention of missing out the first two stations at Scremerston and Goswick, but at the former I relented and followed the signpost along a wide suburban road. Soon I was back on the A1 and, without any remorse at having missed the station, decided to stick to the planned itinerary. I passed the turn-off to Chiswick where, near the end of the road, the tiny settlement of Goswick, some distance past the station, looks out over the North Sea. After quite a distance I turned off towards **Beal**, stopping in a field gateway just past the level crossing. Nothing of any real interest remained, so I climbed over a fence and made for higher ground in a field to get a more general view. **21** Before continuing, I drove to the end of the road at a rough car park beside the marshes opposite Holy Island; the causeway across is only open for a few hours on either side of high tide.

Back on the A1, and taking another turn to the left down a winding lane, I came to the level crossing by **Smeafield** station, where the station house (part of the station itself) was in good condition with a lovely garden and tidily mown grass verges close by the crossing. **22**

Journeying south again, the A1 now bypasses Belford, which, being the largest place between Alnwick and Berwick, had a large imposing station, now a listed building.

Taking a side road off the A1, I stupidly mistook the old crossing-keeper's cottage to the north of the station to be the station house. This inexcusable error was noticed later in the day when, in a book, I saw a photograph of the building, so with a picture of a crossing-keeper's cottage in my camera (see page 4) I drove on to **Lucker**, conveniently on the road to Bamburgh. Here, opposite a large cornfield, was another country cottage, once the station house with a gateway into the old goods yard, now completely naturalised but still with traces of coal at intervals. I took a photograph from the cornfield where the straw, now baled, provided a vantage point. **23** Before I left, the barriers came down and a southbound train thundered over the crossing, which, as with all crossings in the area, had its original station name displayed.

The road to Bamburgh is dominated by the huge castle built on an outcrop of rock on the edge of the village. A number of tourists ambled along the village street, which went downhill with the castle rising menacingly above. I stopped for some refreshment as by now it was almost noon and the morning was warming up at last. On my way along the coast road to Seahouses I parked and walked through the dunes where the Farne Islands lay just out to sea.

In **Seahouses** I parked a short distance from the centre and walked down to and along the harbour, where the tide was out.

▲◄ **21** Beal station, looking west across the main line in 1996, and on 11 June 1960

▼ **22** Smeafield station

▲ **23** Lucker station site, showing the entrance to the coal yard

E. E. Smith

▲▼ **24** Seahouses station, with a train for Chathill in the summer of 1951, and the shed site in 1996, now occupied by a toilet block

▲ **25** North Sunderland station

Opposite the town centre is an enormous car park, once the terminus of the North Sunderland Light Railway. The dilapidated engine shed once stood against the road, but I guessed from my observations that a toilet block now occupied the site. **24** I explored the car park but could find no trace of the light railway. Just inland, at the branch's intermediate station at **North Sunderland**, some original fencing remained, while some free-range hens and ducks occupied the area bordering the old platform. **25**

With thoughts of the return journey now starting to form, I drove inland through lanes, passing through the small farming community of **Newham**, where the station, closed in September 1950, lay only a mile north of Chathill, and at the level crossing a newish bungalow now stood on the station site. **26**

The nearest way to Chathill was to return the way I had come before again driving inland. It came as a surprise to find that **Chathill** station was still open. The signal box,

▼ **26** Newham station

presumably still in use, stood just to the north of the level crossing on the west side. The large listed station building was out of use and in need of some urgent repairs, but across the tracks the old wooden waiting shelter appeared to be in good condition. **27** Any revenue from this station must come from the Seahouses area, as Chathill and its surrounding area has a very sparse population.

The road now led south to Fallodon, where a closed station was marked on my Ordnance Survey map, but is not listed in the 'usual' publications, which is a bit of a mystery. The road crossed the railway on a skew and I pulled into a field gate just past the crossing to have a rest and some refreshment. **28** Across the road was a wooded area and, lurking unseen, Fallodon Hall, whose residents, in times gone by, must have used the station. Several trains hurtled by as I enjoyed the quiet summer's day, while a family, crossing the

▲▼ **27** Chathill station level crossing and signal box, and the waiting shelter on the southbound platform

▲28 Level crossing at Fallodon, looking north

▶29 Christon Bank station

◀30 Little Mill, with a platelayers' hut and the overgrown goods yard beyond

railway on cycles, had to hurry due to the distance between the barriers.

I moved on to **Christon Bank**, only a short distance to the south. Just north of the level crossing the station buildings were still occupied, but next to the crossing an unusual building, possibly of goods shed origin, had been left to its own devices. **29** A pleasant old inn stood a short distance from the crossing, but with much still to do I was keen to continue.

After 4 miles I came to **Little Mill**, where I became the object of attention of a Railtrack crew parked on the other side of the crossing. Soon they were on their way, but with closed-circuit television cameras at every crossing I had to behave in a reasonable way as my progress south had no doubt been observed by someone afar! With the station to the north of the crossing long gone, the only building left was a platelayers' hut just to the south by an area of trees, which, judging by the fencing, had once been the goods yard. **30**

Driving south again I came to Longhoughton and stopped by the rail overbridge to the south of the village. Here, try as I might, I couldn't find a vantage point to take a photograph. The station house, built near the roadside, was of an unusual design and was situated right in the shadow of the overbridge.

I was pleased to arrive at **Alnmouth** half an hour early. After more refreshment in the countrified station car park, where several families had come to pick blackberries, I had a look at the modern station building, which, although quite small, was well designed. **31** Next I followed my Shed Directory, first up the approach road and over the bridge before turning along a pathway at the rear of some railway cottages, which caused some consternation to a group of young people engaged in cleaning a car. I passed through a small gate at the end and descended a flight of concrete steps to the shed yard which, although overgrown, was still worth the effort of trying to locate the engine pits amongst the herbage. I returned the way I had come and, before leaving, climbed the new footbridge. The station master was making his way down the platform towards me, making me wonder if I had been spotted looking over the shed site. We exchanged greetings and at 2.15pm I began the long haul southwards feeling sure that ensuing 'missions' would not be as straightforward or as satisfying.

▼ **31** Alnmouth station, looking north, with the junction for Alnwick curving away through the valley and the engine shed site on the left

EPISODE 4
EAST COAST TO NEWCASTLE

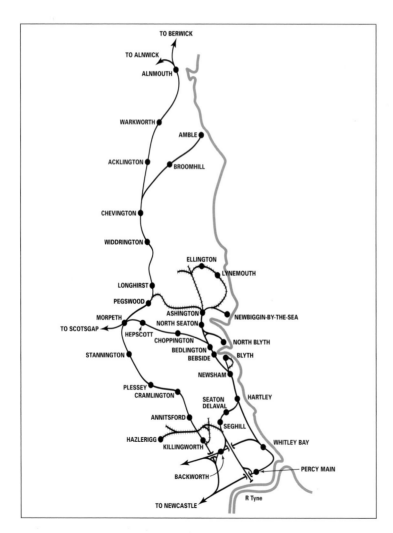

TO BERWICK

TO ALNWICK

ALNMOUTH

WARKWORTH

AMBLE

ACKLINGTON

BROOMHILL

CHEVINGTON

WIDDRINGTON

ELLINGTON

LYNEMOUTH

LONGHIRST

PEGSWOOD

MORPETH

ASHINGTON

NEWBIGGIN-BY-THE-SEA

TO SCOTSGAP

NORTH SEATON

HEPSCOTT

CHOPPINGTON

NORTH BLYTH

BEDLINGTON

STANNINGTON

BEBSIDE

BLYTH

NEWSHAM

PLESSEY

CRAMLINGTON

SEATON
DELAVAL

HARTLEY

ANNITSFORD

SEGHILL

HAZLERIGG

KILLINGWORTH

WHITLEY BAY

PERCY MAIN

BACKWORTH

R Tyne

TO NEWCASTLE

▶ 1 Chevington station

▶ 2 Acklington station

74

8 March 1997

I t was on a cloudless morning in early
March that I again took to the road with
the intention of exploring the mining area of
the Northumberland coalfield. Due to the
intensive nature of the tour I had prepared an
itinerary that I had every confidence in
maintaining. The area to be covered included
the East Coast Main Line between Morpeth
and Alnmouth and the area to the east, from
Amble southwards to Whitley Bay.

It was late morning and pleasantly warm as
I arrived in the area to the west of Amble,
coming to the ECML and a station that proved
to be **Chevington**. I soon regained the use of

my legs in walking the short distance back to
the level crossing, to find that, as with many of
the stations in this area, the station house was
incorporated as a major part of the station
building. Size-wise, the stations on this section
of the main line were either prodigious or of a
much more modest construction. Here was the
latter, and with a large back garden and
peaceful situation – trains excepted – it stood
opposite the site of the closed goods yard with
a massive stop-block near the entrance, while
across the road the brick base of a signal box
remained beside the crossing. **1**

I continued northward and, rounding the
apparently new prison at **Acklington**, passed
through the village and shortly came to the

station, which still 'receives trains'. **2** By now the sun was beating down and the residents of the station and revamped extended goods shed were either gardening or 'taking the spring air'. Some drab industrial units lay on the south side of the pedestrian access road to the platforms. Across the tracks was a disused wooden waiting shelter while, on the near (northbound) side a small Railtrack gang was carrying out some minor platform repairs. **3**

I walked to the roadbridge to the north before heading away on a circuitous route to Warkworth, about 3 miles to the north. I drove down lanes and, soon after crossing the River Cognet, in a pleasantly wooded valley, the road turned north into open farming country. Soon I came to the old trackbed of a colliery branch, which left the main line to the south of Warkworth and had served several mines in its 7-mile climb to Newton-on-the-Moor, roughly marking the northern boundary of the coalfield. Here I paused for a couple of sandwiches in the warm sunshine as I looked eastward towards the coast and the town of Amble. I turned towards the coast, crossing and re-crossing the branch until I came to the now closed station at **Warkworth**, a country facility on a grand scale, quite befitting of the 'seat' of an area manager, while the village, about a mile further on, had all the hallmarks of a medieval town that had not yet entered the 20th century. **4, 5**

◄**3** Acklington station, looking north on 5 July 1959 and in 1997

P. B. Booth

▶ **4** Warkworth station building

▼ **5** Warkworth station, looking
north on 5 July 1959, and in 1997

P. B. Booth

▲▼ **6** Amble station circa 1950, and the site in 1997

I entered **Amble**, a quiet unpretentious fishing village, and parked near the harbour. Here I had some more to eat before I set off to find the station site, which turned out to be just round the corner. I then compared the present view with one dated 1969 in a book, and was able to compare things like roofs, roof windows and even TV aerials. The line now provides a green 'corridor' as far as a building site, which has inevitably been seized upon by a developer. **6**

I walked back to the car via the harbour and set off for Hauxley, a small mining community about a mile to the south. I did not pause there longer than it took to observe

some areas of waste ground that looked to have mining origins, as any remains of the old colliery branches had been discreetly swept away.

As a matter of routine I had checked my next move when I arrived at Hauxley, and only then noticed that there was an intermediate station on the Amble branch at Broomhill, at a point where the colliery lines diverged. This would have to be fitted in to the schedule, but with time in hand there was no great urgency at this stage. A few minutes later I arrived at Broomhill, but there seemed no obvious crossing point of the railway over the main road. I drove behind an old factory

▶ Amble station and harbour

WARKWORTH HARBOUR

to find a large expanse of railway land at the junction, while the adjacent coal-mine site was a ploughed field. Returning to the main road I quizzed a man walking his dog, and he remembered the line in operation and was able to impart some interesting information.

I set off inland along a new road following the route of the Amble branch and re-crossed the main line at Chevington station. I was now embarking on another divergence from my itinerary, which turned out to be a 'wild goose chase'. Without thinking I had assumed the sign 'Causey Bridge', just off the A1, to be the Causey Arch, which on arrival I immediately realised was on the other side of the Tyne! On the way, having taken a wrong turning, I drove along a narrow lane that ended in a farmyard where I was watched by a group of ostriches as I sought re-direction. I again headed towards the coast and through the village named **Widdrington** Station. Two trains had crossed at the station, of modest

◄ 7 Widdrington station

▼ 8 Newbiggin-by-the-Sea station
on 5 August 1955 and the site in

proportions considering the size of the village, before I walked along the platform, which had been raised almost 2 feet due to years of re-ballasting. **7** Alongside the down platform the remains of the goods yard carried a heavy covering of vegetation.

I turned south then east to the mining village of Lynemouth on the coast. I drove through the outskirts of this typical mining community, and although very remote from the main-line railway system, the large modern colliery there was still rail-connected. Alongside was the new-looking power station, where I parked under the railway bridge a short distance from the gatehouse. Several diesel shunters were at work and a modern engine shed stood on the embankment top just down from the bridge.

I had some more to eat before leaving for **Newbiggin-by-the-Sea** where, having been somewhat misdirected, I searched in vain for clues in an area of tumbledown garages at the rear of the Railway Inn before finding the

station site, a pleasant green open space in the south of the town. **8** Only a short distance to the west the goods line from Ashington to Lynemouth could just be seen passing a derelict colliery. As with Amble I had a photograph to compare the changes since closure.

I returned inland towards Ashington and soon after crossing the railway pulled into a quiet side street to get my bearings, as I was using an old OS map. I asked for directions to the station, and after a short walk along the High Street I crossed the railway, which cuts through the centre of the town. Below the bridge on the north side was a signal box, which controlled the junction of the Lynemouth line with that to Ellington Colliery, while to the south the empty station platforms remained in the shadow of a large supermarket.

I returned to the car and took the Ellington road, soon coming to a level crossing over the

▼ Lines around Ashington

aforementioned colliery branch which, on a falling gradient, disappeared into the distance towards the colliery. **9** Just to the south-east was a large expanse of disused land, once a large mining complex that stretched right across the north side of Ashington.

By now it was 3.30pm and I drove to **North Seaton,** about a mile to the south on the north bank of the River Wansbeck. Here a signal box controlled the crossing, but any remains of the station on the north side had been removed. **10** About half a mile further on the road crossed the bottom of the valley and the railway viaduct over the river came into view. The 400-yard-long wrought iron (Belah-type) structure crossed the valley at a high level some distance to the east.

By now, as I was somewhat ahead of schedule, I decided to visit several stations to the south of Morpeth in the last hour before sunset. But first I returned northwards to Longhirst, the station to the south of

Widdrington, where the prodigious station building owed its former existence to the gentleman who resided in the hall of the same name about a mile to the west. The station was surrounded by tall trees and almost warranted a gatehouse of its own. Just to the south, **Pegswood** station, my next stop, lay on the edge of the village and was still open. The original platforms remained, bordered by the usual row of a mixture of pine and deciduous trees. **11**

Continuing south, it was now 5.00pm and I was in a stationary queue on the edge of Morpeth when I saw a sign for the guest-house where I was to stay the night. I was tempted to call it a day, but instead continued, albeit slowly, towards the A1 just to the south of the town. **Stannington** station was conveniently signposted off the A1, and although closed the station house had survived. Two trains passed over the crossing as the sun was sinking fast. **12**

◀**9** Looking south along the mineral line north of Ashington

◀**10** North Seaton level crossing and signal box

► **11** Pegswood station

▼ **12** Stannington station

I hurried on, and while negotiating a short length of old dual-carriageway road I realised that I had passed the turning to Plessey station; located off a very narrow lane, it owed its existence to Plessey Hall just to the north. It was too late in the day to turn back, so I continued to **Cramlington** station, now a modern commuter station with a car park and a curious goods shed-type building by the entrance. **13** The whole area here is a maze of new estates built around the old village centre. I was going to call a halt here as light was fading, but at the last minute I stopped

the car, put the window down and enquired the way to Dudley (Northumberland). With directions I drove south towards Newcastle and came to the small township where the station, known as Annitsford, was named after the village a little to the east of Dudley. The line here is on an embankment and the station, closed in 1958, had been completely removed. Feeling relieved that the working part of the day was over, I was pleased to park right outside my guest-house by 6.00pm. After feasting on fish and chips, I walked to Morpeth station and watched

▲ 13 Cramlington station, looking south on 31 July 1966, and from the road side in 1997, showing the surviving goods shed

several trains pass at only 50mph due to the infamous curve at the south end. The one that did stop was full of people in the usual semi-conscious state, seemingly an effect of today's high-speed rail travel! I returned down the winding hill, over the river and through the town before venturing into an inn just round the corner from the guest-house.

9 March 1997

At 7.30 the next morning, with the weather exceedingly grey, I set off from the guest-house and walked through the quiet streets before crossing the river on Telford's bridge and ascending the winding hill up which I had driven the afternoon before. Passing an old inn, a gentleman out walking his dog gave me directions to the 'Wansbeck Valley' route; about half a mile further on a seemingly unnecessary dip in the road signalled the former crossing point of the line from Reedsmouth Junction.

14 Morpeth (Blyth & Tyne Railway) station frontage, the goods yard, looking north-east with the ECML on the extreme left, and the goods shed, looking south-west

▲ Morpeth station, with the Blyth & Tyne station just south of the NER one

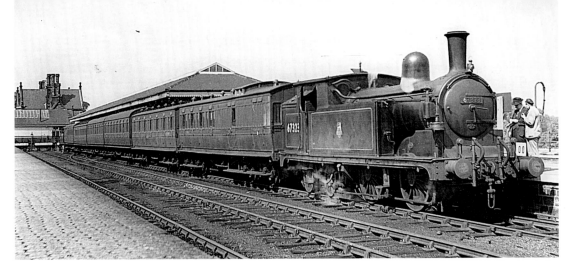

▲▼ **15** Morpeth (Blyth & Tyne) platform on 14 July 1951, and a close view of the station building seen in the background in 1997

Climbing a bank, I saw that the route westwards had been turned into a walkway, while over the road it continued towards the junction with the main line. After a futile walk in the grounds of the cottage hospital that bordered the route, I had to abandon any further incursions and decided to return via the station, as breakfast would be served at 8.30am. I made my way up a bank and through a housing estate, reaching the station with half an hour to spare at 8.00. A railwayman was steadily sweeping up and we exchanged views on the weather before I noticed that I had only two exposures to take before I needed to change the film.

The dark stone of the former Blyth & Tyne railway building, on the south side of the present main-line station, contrasted markedly with the latter's lighter stone, and I used the two exposures on the B&T buildings, intending to stop briefly as I set off after breakfast. **14, 15** A little later I was back at the station after a more than adequate breakfast, and with the gloom showing some signs of lifting I conversed again with the man still engaged in sweeping the platforms, who was still pessimistic about the day's forecast. I took a photograph, then drove the short distance east to **Hepscott** on the line to Bedlington, where the station bordered the small village in lanes about a mile from the main road. Automatic barriers now guarded the crossing, while no trace remained of the platform and the small station building, though nearby was a building that looked old enough to have been the station master's house. **16**

I continued eastward to **Choppington** where there was nothing of interest apart from a nice pub standing next to the level crossing. **17** For the next mile the road ran beside the railway to **Bedlington**, where the route formed a junction with the mineral line to Ashington. I parked in a quiet street bordering the old goods yard and walked across to the disused platform. To the north a signal box lay within the junction, while to the south another box controlled the barriers of the crossing at the south end of the station. **18, 19, 20** I walked along the platform to the small brick-built station building, which was disused and stood on a crossroads in the centre of the town. I returned along the platform and crossed the small goods yard back to the car.

It was quite a cold morning and the skies were still grey as I followed the Ashington line north to Marcheys House crossing, where, just to the south, was the junction of the line from North Blyth. **21** I parked in the village street and walked back to the crossing, controlled by a box on the north side, and looked south across a flat expanse of waste ground stretching from the railway across to a road about a quarter of a mile westward, and to the south for as far as the eye could see.

◀ **16** The site of Hepscott station

▶ **17** The site of Choppington station

18 Bedlington station, the north end on a unknown date probably in the 1950s, with the connection to the colliery on the left, and a closer view of the surviving Bedlington North signal box in 1997

▼ **19** Bedlington station, looking north

▲ **20** Bedlington South signal box   ▼ Bedlington station and colliery

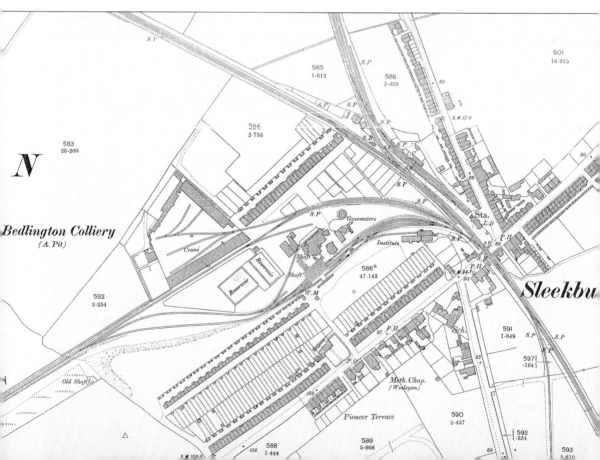

▶ Bedlington Colliery, A Pit, with NCB No 62 shunting in the autumn of 1966

N. Stead

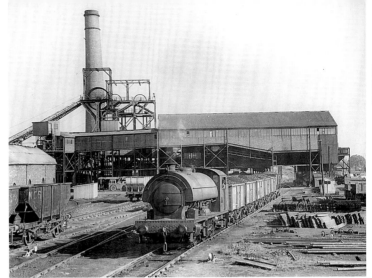

▼ **21** Marcheys House signal box, and the view south from the crossing with the North Blyth line diverging to the left

◀ Blyth and the River Blyth

Back on the road again, I continued towards North Blyth, passing through a wide area of flat land crossed at intervals by goods lines and sidings where massive, brooding buildings looked down across a mixture of slag heaps, power lines and the odd village street. At the coast the road turned southward, alongside deserted beaches, towards **North Blyth**, where I parked opposite the ferry landing stage. The daunting prospect of finding the shed site under an asbestos tip enclosed within an area of car scrapyards and the burned-out ruins of old factories had vanished, as the area was now generally flat and open.

A railway line ran beside the sea wall, while beside a barren waste of reclaimed land lay some terraces of old cottages about half a mile to the south. I left the car and had very soon been shown the actual position of the former shed, which lay adjacent to the railway club. All now became clear as the three rows of cottages were on the map I had of the shed site! I drove along a newly built road beside the sea wall to the old terraces, now an isolated community standing beside the railway club, then walked over the small hillock of grassed made-up ground and thought of my last visit in the early hours of the morning nearly 34 years earlier. **22** Over to the south, across the estuary, lay the town

of Blyth, while the weathered remains of staithes still stood in the muddy creeks, once the scene of wagons teeming coal into the holds of ships. Alongside the river the site of numerous sidings had been levelled, perhaps to be developed if the subsidy to locate here was sufficient. With no pubs and only one corner shop, this small community seemed to be gradually resettling elsewhere.

I left the area, with more environmental disasters passing as factories, and fumbled my way inland. I had to ask the way and after more poring over the map I came to **Bebside**, where I parked along the main road. I walked back towards the crossing and, with nothing remaining of the station, I took a more general view for the record. A white walled inn stood by the crossing, while across the road were the crumbling remains of an industrial estate.

Midday was not far away and, with the low cloud now lifting, I drove into **Blyth**. After being given two sets of directions, I parked in the landscaped grounds of the health centre that now stood on the shed site. **23** On a visit made 20 years earlier, the site was a green open space between two streets, and a further 14 years before that, in a cold grey dawn, the many braziers standing amidst piles of hot

▼ **22** North Blyth, the site of shed 52F (a unique shed code, as it encompassed both North and South Blyth sheds)

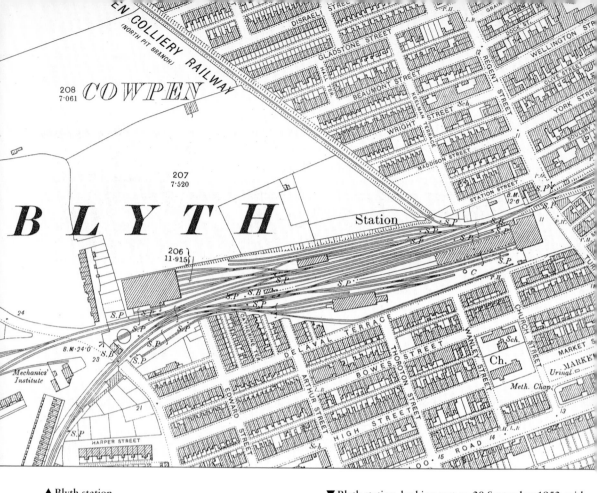

▲ Blyth station

▼ Blyth station, looking east on 20 September 1952, with a passenger train leaving; the shed is on the left

▲ **23** Blyth engine shed site, now occupied by a community hospital

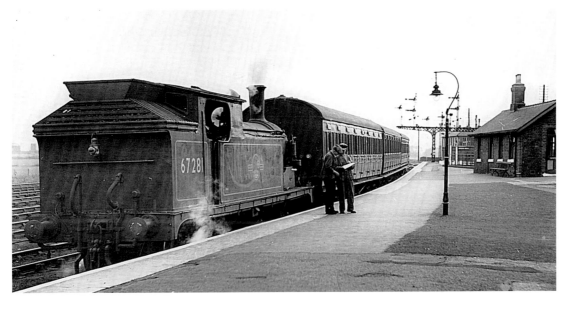

▲▼ **24** Newsham station, with a train for Blyth waiting to leave on 20 September 1957, and the site in 1997, showing the Blyth line diverging to the right

ashes had possibly been of more interest than the engines there! I left the car and, walking to the end of the grounds, passed over the site of the level crossing. As no clear vantage point was available, I returned, but after photographing the health centre I again looked at the site plan and found that the shed site was to the rear of it in the opposite corner of the site. Undaunted I set off again but, as before, although I had pinpointed the shed's position, the high hedge bordering the site made photographing it impossible.

Due to my poor observations I had time to make up, so I set off with some urgency through the now distinctly sunny suburbs to the village of **Newsham**, about a mile to the south. Here I walked along a cinder path beside the end house of a terrace backing on to the railway, and just to the north was the junction of the line to Blyth – which perhaps had been retained as a siding. **24** I was puzzled as there seemed to be no trace of any entrance to the station, but without further ado I took a roundabout route to Hartley.

▲ **25** The site of Hartley station looking east from the Seaton Delaval line; the former 'main line' south to Whitley Bay is beyond the station house

▼ **26** The site of Seaton Delaval station

After a slight 'hiccup' in housing estates in Seaton Delaval, I turned down a lane to the level crossing. After a leisurely break for something to eat I walked back towards the crossing and was soon engaged in difficult conversation with a lady whose Alsatian dog was vigorously trying to effect my disappearance. Hartley had been the junction where the mineral line from Backworth, still extant, had joined the main coastal line from Ashington to Whitley Bay, which has now been lifted. **25** With my nerves now starting to calm and the sky a deep blue, I set off over a field and climbed a small bank opposite the station site, which lay within the junction. Rabbits were scurrying everywhere as I clung to the fence at the top, right opposite the station house, before descending and returning over the field to the gate by the roadside.

With the day now starting to warm up, I continued a mile or so inland to **Seaton Delaval**, walking back to the road bridge and viewing the line disappearing into the distance in both directions. I walked down a cinder path to the luxuriantly overgrown station platforms situated in a cutting to the west of the bridge where I took a photograph. **26**

The weather was perfect as, continuing, I turned right at the crossroads in the town centre. The next station, **Seghill**, was only a mile away, and here I parked by another automatic-barrier level crossing. On the south side were the remains of the station platform opposite a row of old cottages. To the north the line curved from north to east, and on the curve three separate junctions had diverged to

serve a system of colliery railways in the district. **27** The sun shone on a low grassy mound sparsely covered with pine trees, the tell-tale sign of a disused colliery, of which there were many in this area.

Through pleasant open countryside I drove south to Backworth, now an unspoiled country village. Down a side road was a level crossing over the mineral railway I had been following since Hartley. After consulting the map I continued southward and, after crossing the railway, parked in the entrance of a small housing estate. From the overbridge, looking westward towards Newcastle, **Backworth** station had completely disappeared, but the mineral railway that had bridged the main line near the platform ends could just be traced (see the map on page 106). In the opposite direction was the junction of the Hartley and Whitley Bay lines and the earthworks of the Hartley to Percy Main line, which had bridged the line just past the junction. **28**

I had now reached the southernmost part of this tour, and as Backworth was really part of the next one, perhaps something more would be revealed next time. The remaining part of this itinerary was to follow the mineral railway from Backworth village to Hazlerigg, about 6 miles to the west. When planning the tour I had plotted its course on an up-to-date 'A to Z' street map of the area, and found it of great benefit in following the route. I first returned through Backworth village and turned northward along a wide pot-holed road that seemed to have become disused. After quite a distance the road reached its lowest point, and with the surface flooded I set out on foot and

▶ **27** The site of Seghill station, looking north towards the sites of three separate junctions to collieries

▲ The Seatonburn colliery branch running westward towards Wide Open, crossing the ECML, and on the right the branch north from Killingworth to Burradon Colliery

◀ **28** The site of Backworth station, looking east, with the remains of the colliery branch crossing in the distance

soon came to a point where the line I was following crossed a mineral railway heading in the direction of Seghill. **29** With open countryside all around, it continued through a small thicket of gorse, then headed west towards the course of the elevated A19T sweeping southward about half a mile distant.

I returned to the car and bumped my way up to the T-junction and, turning west, came to Camperdown, an older type of village

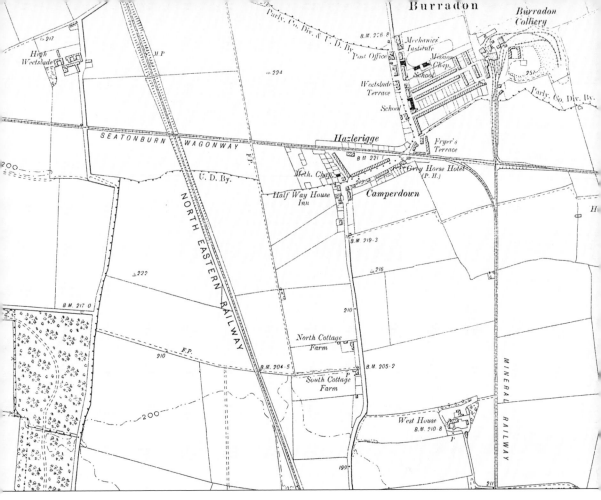

somewhat off the beaten track. I walked back to an area of wasteland that cut through the village centre, once the route of the mineral railway I was following, but unlike many places I visit it was alive with people coming and going, with the two pubs in the centre the focus of attention. Just to the west the line passed over the ECML to the south of Annitsford, but I continued to the village of Wide Open, where again the line crossed a main road on the level. I turned westward

along a country road, and passed the end of Hazlerigg village, where the mineral railway's path could be traced alongside a row of allotments. From here it crossed the road to end at Hazlerigg Colliery, which was also the end of my journey. I drove into a picnic area just off the main road, which had been reclaimed from the remains of the colliery, and spent some minutes reflecting and quietly finished my 'eats' before heading south towards home at 2.55pm.

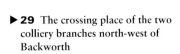

▶ **29** The crossing place of the two colliery branches north-west of Backworth

Episode 5
North Tyneside

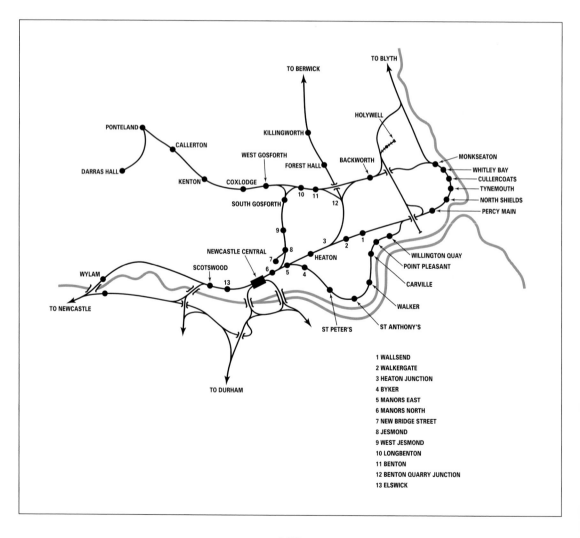

17 May 1997

Spring had passed into early summer as very belatedly one evening I booked accommodation in Cullercoats before quickly packing a bag and sorting out the huge array of books needed for reference purposes. Next morning, having overslept, I set off northward contemplating the 60 sites on my carefully prepared itinerary, but mindful of the daunting prospect of the 9.00pm timed last stop at Monkseaton that evening.

The grey morning was cheerless as, some 20 minutes late, I stopped opposite the station site at Darras Hall, the end of the branch from Newcastle via South Gosforth. It was easily identified as the formation was now a public footpath as far as Ponteland, 1½ miles away, where a reversal had been necessary for trains bound for the city. I walked along the trackbed, passing the station site along a wooded pathway with large houses visible through the trees and the sound of birdsong filling the moist morning air.

I returned and drove to **Ponteland**, a small village surrounded by large prosperous-looking housing estates. As I arrived the railway, now pleasantly grassed over, guided me towards the station site, where there was now a free car park. At first I fumbled my way around the site, not immediately noticing the row of station cottages bordering the car park. **1** These small terraces of about five cottages were all that remained at many of the modernised or closed stations, but more of that later.

I had some coffee and sandwiches before driving south-east in the direction of the city centre. At **Callerton**, the last but one station before Newcastle Airport, on the section

▲▼ **1** Ponteland station in June 1953, and the site in 1997, with the original station cottages off the picture to the right

◄ 2 Callerton station, now Callerton Parkway, looking east down Kenton Bank

▶ 3 Kenton station

relaid from South Gosforth circa 1990, all had been renewed, but I decided that the sudden falling away of the tracks down Kenton Bank was worthy of a photograph. **2**

I continued to **Kenton** station, now called Bankfoot, while following an 'A to Z' map on which I had carefully plotted all the railway routes and station sites in my itinerary. Two electric Metro trains passed as I watched from the level crossing by the modern station. **3**

At **Coxlodge**, now called Fawdon, I was starting to get a little bored until I suddenly noticed a terrace of railway cottages somewhat tucked away behind shrubs adjacent to the platform. **4**

I returned to the car and, after committing

to memory the route to **West Gosforth,** known as Regent Centre since re-opening, I was soon parked in an estate some distance to the north where I was informed by a kind lady that free parking was available at the station. This enabled me to gain valuable time as I had allowed for quite a lengthy walk here and a few minutes later I had parked in the small multi-storey car park built above the station. Descending to street level, I stopped short of entering the station as there were automatic ticket-issuing machines installed, with which I had no intention of getting involved! **5** Both ends of the platforms were, however, visible from road level as the station is situated in a cutting.

I returned to the car half expecting the

J. E. Shelbourn

▲▶ 4 Coxlodge station, looking east on 21 March 1953, in its new guise as Fawdon, looking west in 1997, and the railway cottages alongside

▲ 5 West Gosforth station, now the Metro's Regent Centre station

attendant, snug in his little cabin, to want to inspect my train ticket, but he was nowhere to be seen. It was at this point that I left the remaining section of the line into Newcastle, to be completed the next day, and headed north to **Killingworth**, the station to the south of Annitsford on the main line, where I had reached on my last visit. The only remains there were the brick base of a signal box beside the level crossing. **6** With everything straightforward so far, I set off for George Stephenson's cottage, where he lived for most of his adult life. Unfortunately 'Stephenson House', which I had marked on the map, turned out to be a factory unit on an industrial estate, and it was only after driving around the local roads and drawing a blank

that on my way to the next objective I stumbled upon the cottage. Standing a short distance off the road, it consisted of several stone-built cottages made into one. Round the back, beneath a 'green canopy', was a short length of narrow-gauge track with a 'chaldron' (a small wagon for local transport of coal) placed upon it, depicting the wagonway that used to run behind the house.

After a quick look at the 'A to Z' I left for Forest Hall, the next station to the south. The village centre was busy with people shopping as I parked in the main street. I was unsure of the station site here, as a new road had been built bypassing the town centre. I hastened to the railway overbridge on the new road, which like so many in the area was just too

▼ **6** Killingworth level crossing, with the station site on the right

▶ **7** Holywell, looking north towards Seghill

high to peer over comfortably. Managing with difficulty to do so, I judged the area north of the bridge to be the station site – quite incorrectly, as I was to discover the next day.

With the skies still rather cloudy and showing no signs of improving, I set off for **Holywell**, a short-lived Blyth & Tyne station on the eastern fringe of Backworth village, about 2½ miles to the east. I journeyed along country roads and soon came to the village, which I had passed through on my previous visit to the area without realising that there had once been a station there. After looking north and south along the single line, which followed a straight course on both sides of the level crossing, I settled down to some lunch by two lines of terraced houses, almost certainly built in connection with the railway. **7**

Just before 2.00pm I set off for Backworth station, a mile to the south. Unlike my previous visit, when I had been unable to photograph the station site due to the blazing sun, I was now more concerned about the lack of light as I photographed the scene. Virtually everything here had changed and it was not a place to linger.

Some 2 miles to the south, the two mineral lines that crossed the railway at each end of Backworth station converged on their way to Percy Main and the docks, and a working museum in memory of George Stephenson has been set up, regrettably in a very modern

building. Everything from colliery locomotives to an old NER electric unit was very well displayed in the spacious shed, while the steam railway platform alongside was the starting point for the ride to Percy Main, about 2 miles away, and by 1997 standards the £1 return fare was very cheap.

I had allowed 25 minutes for my next move to St Peter's, on the Riverside branch, some distance towards the city centre. The main roads were more than equal to the task, and with the bonus of the FA Cup Final being played I was soon in a quiet redeveloped area of residential flats alongside the old Riverside branch, which ran on a shelf high above the river as far as Walker. Access to the trackbed was easy, although gauging the actual position, due to landscaping, necessitated some investigation. I made no attempt to exactly locate the station site, since where landscaping or alteration to levels have taken place there is little to be gained by doing so.

The next station, St Anthony's, lay beneath an area of pre-war housing high above the river. Access to the landscaped area was easy and, with a glorious view of the Tyne, I watched several rowing-boats preparing for the following day's competitions on the river.

From here the river bends to the north and I failed to find the site of Walker station, partly due to the main road that now takes a different course and partly due to my looking for a rail

Burn Row

Brierdean Burn

West Row

West Holywell

F.H.

Backworth

Holywell
Square

Meth. Chap.

St. Albe

S.P.

School

Holywell Station
(Goods)

St. John's
Church

Church Street

Thropar Street
Prior Street

Powter Street
Widdrington Street

Institute

Meth.
Chap.

Jack's Row

Gas Works

Backworth
Colliery

Reservoirs

Backworth
Lodge

Lodge

B.M. 203·1

190

200

B.M. 205·8

S.P.

Earsdon Junction

M.P.

S.P.

Earsdon
Square

S.P.

Stoney Row

Meth. Chap.

Moor Edge
P.

S.P.

EAST HOLYWELL COLLIERY RAILWAY

BACKWORTH COLLIERY RAILWAY
(CHURCH PIT BRANCH)

Reservoir
Earsdon Colliery

E A

Abbey Shot Factory

Moor Edge Farm

B.M. 193·6

Earsdon Road

Bertra
B.M.

Whitley Row
F.P.

Ann Street

S.P.

Moor Edge
Ps.

S.P.

S.P.

S.P.

△ 202

Murton Grange
W

Shire Moor

R. C. Chapel

Backworth
Junction

B.M. 227

Backworth Station

North P. West

South P. West

5th

Percy Street

Duke Street
Duchess Street

Church Street

Shiremoor Colliery

Park House

Coast Lane

G.P.

S.P.

CRAMLINGTON COLLIERY RAILWAY

S. Ps.

S.P.

B.M. 239·0

223

N. E. R.

NEWCASTLE TYNEMOUTH & NEWCASTLE

243

BACKWORTH COLLIERY RAILWAY

Old
Quarry

Prospect
Hill

Powder Magazine

John Pit

Holy Stone

Holy Stone
(P.H.)

B.M. 236·1

Parly. Co. Div. & Parly. & Munl. Boro. By.

239

B.M. 236·8

West
Allotment

241

G.P.

B.M. 248·9

The
Allotment

TY

C

TYNES

Parly. Co. Div. & Parly. & Munl. Boro. By.

BLYTH & N.E.R. SECT

G.P.

241

Allotment Mill

Old Wa

233

Allotment Farm

◀ Backworth Junction (centre), Backworth Colliery (top left) and Holywell Colliery (top right)

▲ 8 Willington Viaduct, looking towards North Shields (see the map overleaf)

underbridge instead of an overbridge, a mistake I discovered later. I carried on, driving through an area of old shipyards and large timber-clad warehouses, when suddenly Willington Viaduct came into view, and at the first opportunity I turned up a winding road into a small industrial estate next to a shipyard. **8** From there I set out on foot but failed to determine the route of the line, which, according to the map, seemed to go through the middle of a long warehouse on an embankment! I ducked through a wire fence and on the embankment top was an area of lifted sidings adjacent to a row of houses. Still a little mystified and without any clear indication of the position of Point Pleasant station, allegedly beside the row of houses, I walked the long way round back to the car and was rewarded by a clear view of Willington Viaduct.

After some refreshment I set off for **Willington Quay** station. My enthusiasm was more than starting to wane, as by now my vision was starting to blur with continued use of the small print in the A to Z! However, I found the station site down a short but wide side street with a high tree-clad embankment at the far end. **9**

With no access possible, I drove on to **Percy Main.** On reaching the township, I turned into a housing estate adjacent to the engine shed site and workshops of the Blyth & Tyne Railway. At the far side of the estate the railway had been relaid in connection with the previously mentioned Stephenson Museum project. Bordering the shed site, a stone-built railway building, thought to have been used originally as a drawing office, had been converted into a public house. I left the estate and did not take much persuading that the newly constructed Metro station could be given a miss. For the next 15 minutes I drove on in search of the inn that would indicate the site of the B&T station. After crossing an old railway bridge and enquiring further about this famous local inn, I returned only to pass it on the way back, when I realised it was called the 'Percy Arms', and not the 'Blyth and Tyne' as I had thought. The inn used to afford a view over the platforms from its back upstairs windows, but any signs of the railway had recently been bulldozed away as the land at the rear now bordered a housing construction site. I picked my way through mud as it started to rain and took a photo of the rear of the bespoiled inn, then after a roadside view of the front I drove on. **10**

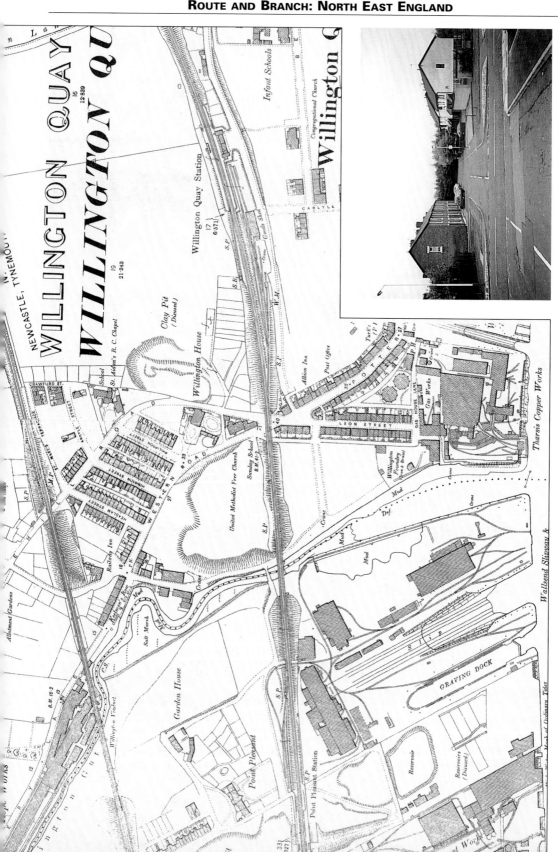

▲ Willington Quay station (right), Point Pleasant station (left), and Willington Viaduct on the Newcastle–Tynemouth line (top left)

▲ 9 Willington Quay station's approach road

▶ **10** The rear of the Percy Arms at Percy Main, disused in 1997

▼ Percy Main shed yard, looking north-east

E. E. Smith

▶ Percy Main staithes sidings, with Hartley Main No 3 (ex-NER No 658) leaving with northbound empties for Seaton Delaval

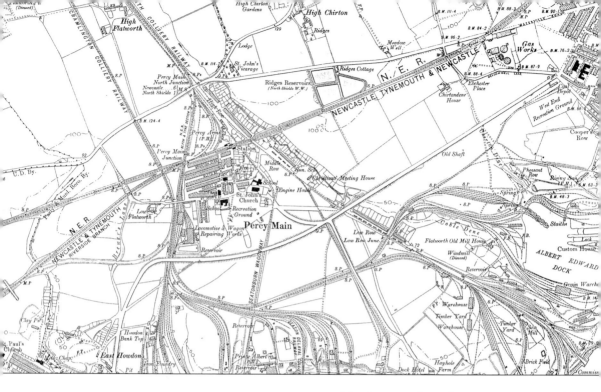

▲ Percy Main

The large station in the centre of North Shields was being brought up to date. With turnstile barriers in place, I did not descend to the station platforms, where the line, at the east end, entered a tunnel beneath the town's streets. I stood by an old wall beside the railway and drank some coffee while planning my next move.

I had no set plan of campaign on arrival in **Tynemouth**, but having parked in a road near the present station I set off on foot to the two early B&T station sites. It was further than anticipated, but on arrival I found the original site had recently been developed under housing, although the retaining walls by the

▼ 11 Tynemouth, showing the site of the original B&T station

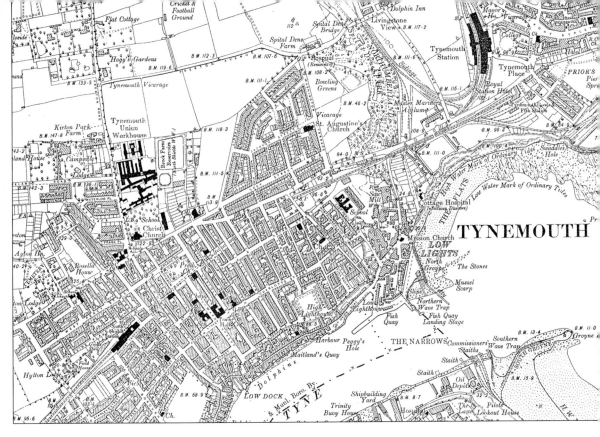

▲ North Shields station (bottom left) and Tynemouth
station (top right) – a continuation of the map opposite

roadside had survived. A high footbridge
across the Metro line provided a good vantage
point. **11** I did not seek out the B&T
temporary station, but noted the spur to the
later B&T station running under a nearby
road in a cutting.

With rain now falling I passed the imposing
B&T station master's house and returned
along the main road, getting steadily wetter by
the minute. On reaching the car I grabbed an
umbrella and set off again, first to the present
station with its overall roof, much ornate
ironwork and wide concourse, where piles of
debris were being assembled by a group of
teenage cleaners using large brooms. The long
impressive stone-built frontage was in better
condition than the overall roof, under which I
found my umbrella to be most effective! **12**
Retracing my steps past the car I soon noted
the later B&T station (now a TA drill hall) on
the corner of the main road; this most
impressive building closed in 1882 when the

present station was built. I crossed the main
road in search of the Newcastle & North
Shields Railway (N&NSR) station, 1847-82,
but came to no firm conclusions – more on
that later.

Back at the car, I changed my wet coat and
drove to Cullercoats, where I did not seek out
the B&T station as it seemed to have been
overtaken by suburbia. The NER station, a
short distance away and of a rather basic
design, was now on the Metro line.

It was still raining heavily, and after a
quick look at **Whitley Bay** station with its
appealing frontage and high, grand clock
tower, I drove on to **Monkseaton**, parking in
the road by the station. **13** I had spent some
time researching the changes to the system in
the Monkseaton area, and as the rain had
now stopped I had a brief look round and
noted the line of the B&T route (just east of
the present station) before leaving for a well-
earned rest at my night's accommodation,
with the intention of either returning later
that evening or next morning before
breakfast. The guest house was comfortable

▲◀ **12** Tynemouth NER station, exterior and interior

▶ Cullercoats station, looking north towards Whitley Bay in 1938

▲ **13** Monkseaton NER station

▶ **14** Tynemouth, the former N&NSR station

and my room overlooking the sea was a welcome relief from driving.

With my coat and shoes drying on the radiator, I 'recharged my batteries' and later drove back into Tynemouth, parking near the first B&T station. Further incursions revealed nothing new, so I drove back to the area of the N&NSR station. Here I discovered the 1847 station – the listed building was in use as

living accommodation. **14** Much pleased by this discovery, I returned to Cullercoats and the guest house and, after a short rest, walked back into Tynemouth, taking an umbrella with me as a precaution. The evening remained dry, but there was little to choose between the pubs in the town, which were packed solid. Towards 10.00pm I returned along the seafront to my accommodation.

18 May 1997

Overnight the sea mists had edged inland, with the sea barely visible from my window as, at about 6.30am, I began to tidy my disorganised bedroom. Any early forays were quickly ruled out and I left soon after 8.00am, driving inland to Wallsend with visibility improving all the time. Heading south off the main road to Newcastle I came to an area near the docks, once the site of Carville station on the Riverside branch. A rough expanse of ground bordering the shipyard lay in front of me and the brick base of a signal box stood by the roadside.

The nearby Wallsend Metro station appeared to be a totally new construction, so I pressed on towards **Walkergate**. This was similar to Wallsend, although some original retaining walls survived, and an old warehouse stood alongside. I took the time to climb the steps up to the platform, where all was clean and tidy. **15**

Soon things started to go wrong as I became quite lost somewhere in Heaton. Eventually, after considerable difficulties, I managed to plot a course for Heaton engine shed, which to my annoyance was only a stone's throw from my last stop at Walkergate. A new station (Chillingham Road) had been built at the end of a cul-de-sac off the main road and was hemmed in by factory buildings. From the footbridge over the tracks the large expanse of

Heaton Junction, with its new diesel depot and marshalling yards, lay before me, but the precise location of the old 52B Heaton engine shed appeared to be under some running lines. **16** I returned to the road bridge at the top of the yard, over which I could clearly remember peering at about 6.00am on a dull morning some 34 years earlier, and surprisingly there did not appear to be a great deal of change.

About half a mile nearer the city centre I parked by a row of decaying buildings that passed as shops in the centre of an area of back streets, but now without their local station, **Heaton**, in the deep cutting in the lee of a long overbridge. **17**

Less than 200 yards away lay the site of Byker station, but hidden in an area of ruinous back streets. Driving a little nearer the 'target zone' I stopped where an old street was cut off by a present-day primary route. Armed with my up-to-date 'A to Z' and my camera I proceeded to try and fathom out the whereabouts of Toward Street, made even more difficult as the remnants of old streets generally bear no name signs. I paced up and down for perhaps 5 minutes, quite hopelessly, before walking somewhat more positively along an old street where, at the end behind an old wall, the site of Byker station lay in the mangled remains of a cutting – the railway appeared to have entered a tunnel beneath where I was standing.

◀ **15** Walkergate station

▲▼ **16** Heaton Junction, with a westbound goods leaving and the shed on the extreme right in the junction, and the new station, known as Chillingham Road, in 1997

The last hour had presented all sorts of difficulties, but I still had time in hand. My next objective was Ouseburn Viaduct, which I had seen from a distance only a short time before. I set off along the aforementioned primary route and was able to stop in a side street only a short walk past the viaduct. Built to the same design as Willington Viaduct, with seven metal arches on stone piers, Ouseburn is slightly shorter, at 306 yards. High above the

valley on the modern road bridge I looked across to the eastern end of the viaduct where, far below me, sheep grazed in a small green hollow set amidst old walls and tumbledown ruins, with the Ouseburn flowing underneath between the viaduct piers. **18**

Back in the car, I perused the 'A to Z' to gauge the route of Newcastle's **Quayside branch**, which, with gradients of 1 in 30, left the main line near Manors East and descended

▲▼ **17** Heaton station, looking east on 17 August 1959,
and looking west across the site from the station
overbridge in 1997

◀ **18** Ouseburn Viaduct from the

▲ Heaton Junction and shed (top right), Heaton station (centre), and Ouseburn Viaduct (bottom left)

mainly in tunnels to the quayside. However, with much new building evident, I had little hope of finding any of the short cuttings where the line emerged between the tunnel sections. Continuing without success, I was lucky to park near the quayside on the road leading up to the city centre. **19** There was much activity on the river as the rowing competition was about to start. I walked amongst a glut of new buildings with 'Olde Worlde' paved precincts, some still under construction. I was most intrigued by the appearance of a 'tunnel mouth' almost opposite where I'd parked. with an apparent dark sooty mark above. **20**

With this in mind, I set off again driving up the hill into the centre before parking near

where the ECML rides high across the short gap over Dean Street. I took a photograph and, there being little traffic about, did a swift U-turn in the road, aiming to relocate about a quarter of a mile to the north. A couple of minutes later I unintentionally entered a multi-storey car park after getting away from traffic lights in the wrong lane! So, about midday, I set off into the city, first walking southward to **Carliol Square**, the terminal station of the Newcastle & North Shields Railway before the opening of Newcastle Central. The centre of the square was now built on, leaving just three streets and the motorway around its perimeter. At the south-east end an open yard showed good indications of the former presence of the railway, while just up the street the bus depot, once the site of the goods yard, now provided shelter for other road vehicles. **21**

◀ **19** Newcastle Quayside on an unknown date, probably in the 1950s, and the less industrial ambience in 1997

▶ Newcastle-upon-Tyne, showing Central station (centre bottom), Manors station to the east, and above it the former New Bridge Street station and the line to Jesmond station (top right). Bottom left is Forth Banks goods station, site of the former Newcastle & Carlisle Railway station. (Note that the King Edward Bridge over the Tyne, south-west of Central station, has not yet been built.)

▼ **20** Newcastle Quayside, showing the possible site of the Quayside tunnel mouth

◄ **21** The site of the N&NSR station at Carliol Square, Newcastle

►▼ **22** Manors station, with a southbound mineral train passing through on an unknown date, and the station, looking west, in 1997

I then walked east, coming to an abrupt halt beside the urban motorway running north to south into the centre. I 'took to the air', crossing a high-level footbridge until the Metro station at Manors North came into view. Alongside were some remnants of the railway to the north of the old **Manors North** station, with an old bridge and ballasted trackbed beneath, set amidst some newly landscaped pedestrian walkways. Wondering whether I should continue further on or head north in search of New Bridge Street, I crossed the bridge, then went back to take a photo of the site of the old Manors North station. Soon I realised that the area about 100 yards to the

north-east was New Bridge Street, the old headquarters of the Blyth &. Tyne Railway. Things were becoming a little clearer now, especially after I had walked south for a short distance to a bridge over the railway, and looking west were the remains of **Manors East** station and the more distant curve into Newcastle Central. **22**

I now turned my attentions to **New Bridge Street** and the large area of land to the north. The area now comprises a cinema with a massive car park attached. **23** I walked north along a suburban avenue with the substantial boundary wall of the goods yard on my left. At the top of the yard a single electrified spur

▶▼ **23** The site of Newcastle New Bridge Street station, showing the frontage replaced by a cinema, and the platform area, looking south in 1997, now a large car park

24 Jesmond 'Old Station', an inn in 1997

25 West Jesmond station

off the Metro line at Jesmond passed beneath a new block of flats before threading its way between the motorway and the car park. I returned across the motorway on another footbridge, with a widespread view of the whole area, before walking through some pleasing old streets back to the car park. That in effect completed the city centre.

My next objectives were the stations between Manors North and Benton Quarry Junction, going first north then east through the outer suburbs. I took the first exit off the urban motorway and parked just round the corner from a railway bridge. This was Jesmond, and on the opposite side of the railway was the Metro station and the spur to New Bridge Street at the north end. I crossed the main road and continued parallel to the railway to **Jesmond** Old Station, a listed building that was now an inn, standing at the south end of the Metro station platforms. **24**

Just to the north-west, West Jesmond station still retained some of its original buildings, built in brick to a design similar to Cullercoats. **25**

With the A to Z proving its worth, I drove parallel to the railway to South Gosforth, a mainly new station, where, like several others, the only original remains were the road bridge and the walls to the platform. I drove through the town centre and turned into a lane to emerge in a housing estate opposite the present South Gosforth depot, which, before the Metro, had been used to maintain DMUs. Here I took a 15-minute break away from the traffic and busy roads. I had parked almost opposite the gatehouse, but walking over a green bank alongside the depot a sudden break in the vegetation revealed the impressive frontage of the building and the quiet yard with its grass-grown tracks.

Returning, I drove the short distance to

▲ 26 Longbenton station

▶ 27 Benton station

Longbenton station passing through the housing estate on its north side. From a bush-lined path I climbed some steps of recent construction and was further impressed by the well-planned ramp access for wheelchairs that circled overhead. The pleasing frontage of the station, built in more recent days to serve the older estate on the south side, had all its original buildings intact. **26**

I drove on to **Benton** and found there a large but now basic building with a curving road entrance and station master's house on the north side. **27**

The afternoon was becoming brighter, and having decided that the only road access to Benton Quarry Junction was on the north-east side (I was on the south-west side) I set off towards Forest Hall where I had stopped the day before. I turned down Station Road and it

soon became clear that I had misjudged the position of the station the day before, as this was the site of the level crossing at the south end of the station. The short road is now a cul-de-sac, and the crossing has been replaced by a new road bridge over which I had looked with difficulty not 24 hours before. I talked with an old gentleman who had lived in the area since the 1930s and who was pleased to impart some of his long-cherished memories of the line.

I drove on, now in familiar territory, and turned down a side road that soon became a track. Setting off on foot I came to **Benton Quarry Junction**, where the Metro line to Monkseaton bridged the ECML. **28** I watched trains from a meadow bounded by trees before taking the track back to the car.

It was now time to relocate from the north-

▲◀ **28** Benton Quarry Junction, looking north on an unknown date, and the crossing of the ECML by the Monkseaton line in 1997

east to the west of Newcastle to see a little more of the former Newcastle & Carlisle Railway. In the end I plumped for the route through the city centre to reach Elswick, about 3 miles west of Newcastle Central. In more recent years the railway between Scotswood and Central station has closed, and the route now follows the southern bank of the Tyne as it did when the line was first built. On reaching the river at **Elswick** I stopped just to the east of where the railway crossed to the south of the main road, which it followed all

the way into the city. Looking over a long wall that bordered the railway, I saw what appeared to be the platform foundations of Elswick station on a wide shelf just above the river. **29**

Driving towards the city, I passed the site of the Vickers-Armstrong and Armstrong-Whitworth engineering factories, which once stretched for 2 miles along the north bank of the Tyne and were known as Elswick Works. Turning off the main road I noted a sudden widening of the formation, which for much of

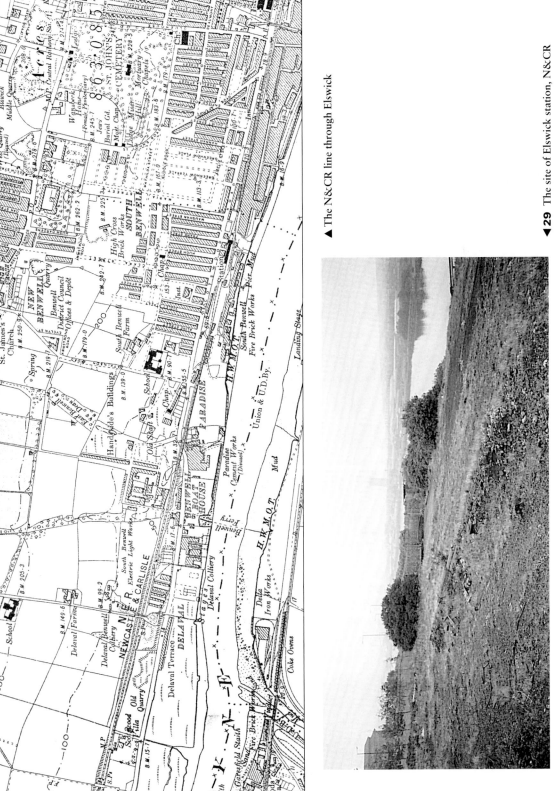

▲ The N&CR line through Elswick

▼ **29** The site of Elswick station, N&CR

▲ **30** In the area of Shot Tower, the former terminus of the Newcastle & Carlisle Railway, 1839-47

▼ **31** Forth Banks, the site of the former N&CR terminus, 1847-50

its way into the city was on an embankment flanked by solid stone retaining walls. From 1839 to 1847 the terminus of the N&CR was at Shot Tower, and I came to the conclusion

that I was not far away but could not risk climbing to track level due to obstructions on the embankment side. **30**

I drove to the far end of Railway Street and

▲ **32** Newcastle Central station

▶ **33** Newcastle Central station,
showing the water tower and
engine shed site

set off on foot, finding a convenient flight of
steps to gain access to the new Redheugh
Bridge across the river. Although I had only
recently crossed the bridge, I was now able to
interpret the remains of **Forth Banks**, the
terminus of the N&CR from 1847 to1850.
The site once housed three engine sheds and a
goods depot, and on looking down I saw the
remains of an island platform and a goods
shed among the brick-strewn wastes. **31** The
sliding side doors of the goods shed were now
below ground level on the north side with the
extension of the railway into **Central** station.

I returned to the main road and walked the
short distance to Central, entering by the huge

portico, and was pleased to note that repair
work, in progress on my last visit, had been
completed. **32** Crossing the bridge to the
south side, I noted that the old water tower
was in good condition; it dated from the days
when there were two engine sheds at the
station, before the NER moved out to Forth
Banks in the 1870s. **33**

I took a last look at the east and west ends
of the station before returning to the car at
Forth Banks. The journey home was swift
and easy, and what had seemed to be a very
strenuous timetable had been made quite
easy with good planning and the invaluable
'A to Z'.

INDEX OF LOCATIONS